MO~~RE OR~~ LESS AT SEA

The Unusual Tour

Of An Infantry Lieutenant

In The Western Pacific

1945 – 1946

By

AL JENSEN

More or Less At Sea

The Unusual Tour
Of An Infantry Lieutenant
In The Western Pacific
1945 – 1946

by

Al Jensen

1-4196-8868-5
9781419688683

Contents

Introduction

When I boarded the troopship in San Francisco Bay as an infantry replacement officer, I was one of the thousands being shipped into the Pacific Theater to help end the war with Japan.

I had spent the months since graduating from the basic Officer Candidate Course at Fort Benning, Georgia in the cadre of the independent 144th Infantry Regiment. Our mission was advanced infantry training of non-commissioned officers from other branches who had been transferred to the infantry to meet changing needs of the army. At this time, the need was for junior officers and non-coms as replacements for losses during the upcoming final surge into Japan itself.

I was a second lieutenant, platoon leader for an anti-tank company in the training regiment. We were working with 57mm towed anti-tank guns but training in many advanced skills as well. In July 1945, I received overseas orders, along with several hundred other first- and second lieutenants who were sent aboard the SS Cape Mendocino.

The change came suddenly. Our convoy had stopped in Pearl Harbor en route to Manila (though I am not sure we were told that much) when the Japanese capitulated. This left the lot of us, among other thousands, on the way to do nothing for which we were trained.

My memoir, written in 2003 and lightly told, recounts what happened to one young officer in the months following World War II.

Al Jensen

Getting There is Half the Fun

When we climbed down the nets into the bobbing landing craft, we infantry officer replacements were still pretty much at sea. We knew we were in Manila Bay, near the north shore. We still had no idea where we were going, why, or what for after 35 days en route from San Francisco. Our C-5 troopship, the Cape Mendocino, looked smaller as we were marched over to the narrow-gauge railroad near the beach. She disappeared from view as we clambered into the shabby cattle cars. I felt almost, though not quite, as if I were leaving home again. The rails went only north here.

I thought back at our journey so far: Having been assigned to the third-level in a stack of bunks next to the Cape Mendocino's thrashing propeller shaft before we left 'Frisco, I'd opted to spend my days and nights on deck, sheltered beneath a portside 40-millimeter gun tub.

"POSH," quipped one of my former ROTC college mates, "Port out, starboard home." He pointed to the late morning sun, which offered us promise of warmth and tanning exposure.

Only our twice-daily chow lines took us bottom deck, aft compartment lieutenants down into the bowels of the trooper. Traveling in a large convoy from the Golden Gate to Hawaii, the only other ships we met at sea were three U.S. Navy submarines returning from patrol. They had just surfaced and were entering the narrow channel into San Francisco Bay.

Strangely, our greatest danger during the long voyage had come at Pearl Harbor. While we were anchored out in the roadstead, the news came that Japan had capitulated. Every ship and shore battery, indeed every weapon down to .45-caliber automatics and Garand rifles, let fly into the lightless harbor sky. Spent rounds, still-burning flares and tracers hailed all around us as we crowded the deck to watch the celebration. I thought: If there had been this much stuff in the air here on December 7, 1941, this war would have been over long before now!

After another couple of days of wondering what would happen next, the Cape Mendocino and its convoy up-anchored and plodded on toward the southwest at about eight knots. Apparently, we were still going deep into the Pacific Theater, silent and blacked-out from dusk until dawn, a lonely little group of dots on the empty sea. After several days, we found out where we were. The PA system blurted that we had this date crossed both the Equator and the International Date Line, entering the Realm of The Golden Dragon, and the only ceremony would be issuance of appropriate certificates for all hands. Now we knew pretty much where we were, but were not too sure when.

Though the ceremonial trappings were eliminated at our entry into the Realm of the Golden Dragon, the Far East and its ocean, this was a day significant in tradition, I later discovered. "Crossing the

Line" ceremonies are ancient, traced even to the Vikings who lurk somewhere in my own ancestry. The northern seafarers observed line crossings of what is now the Tropic of Cancer. The Greeks, Phoenicians and others gave offerings and obeisance to sea gods at important points in the Mediterranean excursions.

The two greatest line crossings in the Pacific became the Equator and the 180th meridian of longitude, the International Date Line. Each marked one half way around the earth. In the early days, and until flight, relatively few people experienced these crossings.

Crossing the 180th meridian was magic in a unique way: going to the west, a whole day disappeared, was lost from the calendar. Crossing to the east a calendar day was repeated. So Tuesday/Wednesday one way, and then Monday/Monday the other. With regards to the ceremony, the crossing must be by sea for the initiation of the voyager.

With the thousands of Americans who have made the crossing during the nineteenth, twentieth and early twenty-first centuries, the custom has continued. A navy friend tells of his heavy cruiser crossing in 1942 where some 1,300 sailors were initiated in a single ceremony. Only about two hundred of the crew were "shellbacks" to put on the event.

By our convoy course aboard the Mendocino, our certificates recorded our ship's crossing of both the Equator and the International Date Line on the same day. My certificate has the entries "Latitude 0 degrees, Longitude 180 degrees." Only recently I learned that this entitles me to be addressed as a golden shellback as well as a member of the Order of the Golden Dragon. There are, however, no pecuniary benefits.

Of late, having found, ironed, and framed my 1945 Golden Dragon paperwork, I have taken to asking other likely folks whether they too have crossed the International Date Line by sea. More friendships have warmed; truly there is a fellowship of sorts among those who have entered and safely exited the Dragon's realm.

We saw nothing and were told less, but the sun kept shining and so we played Hearts or Pitch and kept our clumsy GI lifejackets handy, and we griped half-heartedly. We knew World War II was over, but did all those Japs? Several bored experts suggested that the government would save a lot of dough if they turned our boat around and returned us directly to Fort Ord for discharge. Some thought Hawaii would be far enough, an even more unlikely scenario. We didn't even know where it was we were supposed to land back when there was a war on. No authority was interested in unleashing our creativity or improving our understanding.

No, we did not have an inkling of what "they" would do with the batch of us, and we wondered if they did. The Honshu invasion where we had expected to be replacements was off, of course. But the troop buildup would keep replacement men and equipment alike streaming into the far reaches of the Pacific for months yet, probably matched by a flow of returning veterans with enough service points in their pockets. We went back to playing cards.

I, for one, had had enough of traveling in our teeming ark by the time we pulled into the big harbor at Ulithi Atoll, which seemed to be a circle of low sand dunes in the midst of an oceanic desert. A few senior officers and crew went ashore for conferences or orders, returning to inform us the blackout was lifted, but little else. Then off we set, heading west-northwest and eventually raising the southern tip of Luzon Island on the starboard bow. As we entered the San Bernardino Strait we encountered our second small group of vessels, another pack of American subs running on the surface. At this time we were certain we were headed for the Manila port, and that the war was over for us, too. And so it had proven.

Fond as I'd always been of fresh-water sailing and boating, I figured the next boat

I'd be on would be a faster, more comfortable troopship, maybe in a year or so, departing Manila for a speedy trip home. Now I mused about this likelihood as we stood waiting to board the lengthy but narrow troop train to somewhere more immediate. Finally, about noon, it clattered to life and slowly backed down our spur, pushing the wooden-slatted, tin-roofed cars next to a makeshift loading platform. Apparently, its consignment of enemy captives from the Luzon Highlands had been offloaded nearby. We boarded with our carbines, pot helmets, and field packs. Our A-bags and B-bags were somewhere else.

This railway car of ours was spartan in all respects. No windows, just paint-worn cattle-car slats, some pretty chewed up, one sliding door centered on each side, suitable for Philippine horses, mules, goats, even water buffalo. Our side door was open; the other had been padlocked shut. Along each side of the car a backless plank bench ran fore and aft. We were to sit facing each other, backs to the view. A third narrow plank ran the length of the center, filling up last as we clambered in no particular order. There was no conductor, no ticket to punch, and no timetable. A soldier slammed the door shut and hooked the hasp closed. It must have been about 1400 hours; the tropical rain turned on, fortunately straight down. We waited.

Toot, toot! Far ahead, we could hear the engine's driving wheels rubbing on the thin tracks, and the clanking of chains and hitches as each car in its turn began to inch along. Finally, our car was jerked into motion, reminding us about the laws of inertia as we clattered gear and cursed the slivered benches. I did not try to guess where we were going, how far, when we might be freed from this cage, or why anything. Replacement life was much different here than had been my enlisted life back in the States.

Eventually the trip smoothed out, at least horizontally. We rolled along, probably at about ten miles per hour, rocking and lurching, squealing and clanking, in the midst of a plume of low-hanging wood smoke. Suddenly the engineer blew his whistle again, three times, and locked the engine's brakes, pounding us to a stop car by car. We on the center bench slid and surged to the front, having nothing to hold onto. Silence. The rain fell, the jungle steamed, and the smells of wet earth, greenery and railroading enveloped us as we sat.

Then we discovered more about military priorities. Another little cattle train plugged by us toward Manila as we lay penned on the siding. It would have been close enough to touch if we'd had windows. Through the slats, we could see each car was crammed with dirty, angry Japanese soldiers. I thought they regretted having surrendered. Judging by their words and motions they were unhappy. And they were headed for home!

Abruptly the rain turned itself off, instantly replaced by blinding sunshine. We learned about tropical heat in jungle clearings. This whole program was repeated throughout the day and evening. But our train did not stop at any depot. We had no food, and almost no water except drippings from holes in the tin roof. We did have steam heat.

Other than the south-bound remnants of the local Imperial Army, we saw a few farmers working in their little paddy-fields, some muddy crossroads over which we rolled without slowing, whistling, or clanging the engine's little bell, various narrow clearings with small shotgun shacks, and a few little boys perched solemnly atop giant carabao. Both animals and kids stared placidly at the clattering troop train.

Long, long after the tropical night dropped leadenly around us, we stopped again, the engine sighed far ahead, and I saw dim flashlights wavering toward us, occasional beams reflecting in mud puddles beside the tracks. Voices rose out of the deeper silence as doors creaked open, releasing the stiff passengers, now again officers and gentlemen after fourteen hours' confinement.

Relatively soon, our own door hasp was unfastened by a military policeman, who ordered us to debark and stand immediately outside. We had no trouble hearing or understanding his rapped-out orders. I climbed out in the first third of the troops, by virtue of having been straddling that middle bench. This was not an honor, but a matter of practicality, since those on both side benches were squeezed against the walls until we moved. Much grunting, groaning and stretching noise came from the deep dark as we waited in some more rain. Now our gear was getting soaked as we pulled out ponchos and fumbled into them.

"Fall in! Form up! Follow me!" a dim figure in a poncho commanded from the direction of the engine. So we did, raggedly stumbling along until we gradually settled into a comfortable route march.

The soggy and slippery footpath widened out into a narrow roadway as we slogged by the dead engine. It seemed to have been abandoned by its crew. The boiler was still steaming a bit here and there at joints. The metal crackled and snapped as it cooled. At some indeterminate distance to our right, we could just make out watery squares of lamplight, the window openings of small buildings huddled under the umbrella of jungle-edge. It was a village, I guessed; certainly not Baguio or the temperate-climate Highlands vacation area.

Moving a little more quickly now, we marched off toward the village square (or maybe crossroads, it being difficult to see that evening). We sloshed along with our carbines slung muzzle-down, the incessant plunging rain rattling on several hundred helmets before cascading down people's necks. Some muttering occurred in the ranks. Blessedly, no one counted cadence. No one sang a popular marching song. No one created waves of laughter with snappy comments. We were going someplace.

For a while we went up (or it may have been down) Main Street of this no-name village. On each side, a few feet from the edge of the muddy track stood several open-fronted shops and business establishments. Most were uncrowded little bars with scratchy wind-up Victrola music and clouds of harsh tobacco smoke. Globules of dim lamplight intensified the surrounding gloom. One popular nightspot boasted a noisy gasoline generator, which powered some flickering DC current light bulbs and a static-laden blast of radio music. In a few smaller storefronts, their proprietors stood behind counters filled with trinkets, glumly watching our silent parade. I saw no civilians except in the bars, no service personnel anywhere. Not yet.

Soon we were passing away through the minimal suburbs, pushing on for a mile or so. Then lights flashing in the road waved us off through a hedge and into a field. I guessed this was an off-season rice paddy, for it was lower, flat, free of brush, and paved with several inches of standing water.

"Fall Out!" came a command. We mostly just stood stupidly around, and then eased silently toward a slightly higher piece of ground to await orders. I cannot remember any whining, but after being awake for 24 hours, my senses were dulled considerably. At last we were stopped.

Coming to life, the army called roll, though who answered any name in the dark was questionable. Order thus established, we were called off into groups of twelve and led to numbered squad tents along a nearby company street. When we went to our billets, our group found a sagging and soaked, tipsy tent, which had been partially pitched in the rice paddy. Inside, a Zippo lighter's flame showed us several small piles of folded canvas cots lying in the water awaiting our assembly. As we each struggled to unfold and stretch out a cot, we found that the wooden end pieces could not be stretched far enough to engage them in the sidepieces. The immersed canvas had shrunk, leaving about four feet of damp cot surface for each man and his gear. This is very funny as I think back. After guying canvas and stakes into the semblance of beds, we turned in, holding assorted equipment in our arms, and gradually dozed off.

Pre-dawn, whistles blew and we assembled for quite an informal reveille, then grabbed mess kits and cups. We alerted to the smell of hot army coffee. Across the way, a small army field kitchen emerged from the mists. Having carried no rations, we were ready for breakfast.

As our breakfast was served we moved in a single column, slowly and orderly, past some tables filled with fresh enough army white bread. I got two chunks. Then we came to washtubs filled with Vienna sausages floating in cold water. A cook dumped a dozen or more of the little slugs into my extended mess kit. Next stop was for coffee, the better part of a quart, already conditioned with powdered milk and ample sugar. No waiting! We ambled back to our tents to enjoy the repast. I have willingly eaten cold Vienna sausages twice in the half century since that breakfast.

Our stay, though brief, was not all bad, and a far better reception than we might have expected if we'd arrived even a few weeks earlier, there in Tarlac, Luzon. Tarlac was the nameless village we had come through, our secret destination. We saw the name on a roadside sign a few days later, as we retraced our midnight walk in broad if damp daylight to the train siding. Maybe it was the same train we had ridden in on. The unmarked engine and cars offered no clue. The engine was now on the other end, headed south. We were going back to Manila itself, to some genuine RepoDepo. Our last action at Tarlac was another roll call. All present and accounted for.

Manila Days

When I landed there in the late days of summer 1945, Manila was just springing back to vigorous free life after a half-decade of war. As the first and largest American city to fall in the Japanese invasion, it had suffered under continuous and brutal occupation, then another battle as the Philippines were freed by waves of Allied attack. My memories of this time are scattered vignettes, for I was sent off on duties elsewhere within a couple weeks.

After our train arrived from Tarlac, we were unceremoniously offloaded again, packed into the backs of GI drab cattle trucks, and hauled off to a replacement depot somewhere near Embassy Row. Before the war this might have been a prestigious Manila address. Now it was a sea of squad tents in rows and columns. Typical Army.

We were assigned to minimal quarters, but all nice and dry, clean, functional for what promised to be a temporary stay. Showers and dining areas were nearby. Luxury, almost. Civilian Filipinos worked as waiters, servers, and clean-up staff. Our duties consisted of being present for daily formations, eating, sleeping, and waiting. Surrounded by many officers, among whom we lieutenants were most in evidence, we found time to be off and sightsee, or at least disappear for hours.

One of the first sights for me was a solitary fire hydrant on a block that had been obliterated in the retaking of Manila. It stood there alone, with one of its arms blown completely away. A slow, steady stream of water bled from the hole, draining off into the debris-cluttered gutter. Women and children were lining up to fill buckets and pans with the clean-looking water.

The city's public transit system seemed to have been eliminated, though burned out wrecks of buses and trolleys abounded along the main roadways we traveled. Instead, a thousand jitneys careened through the streets on hard-to-figure routes. Pre-war civilian trucks, many with GI tires, and a substantial number of liberated Jap vehicles predominated, though already some converted army jeeps were in that throng. Horns blaring and drivers shouting, the jitneys wove in and out through the bicyclists and the horse-drawn wagons. Every driver ignored pedestrians. Suddenly one of the walkers would run, waving, into the roadway to hail a passing jitney. Hardly stopping, it would rush off again full-tilt, with a new paid-for passenger hanging on somewhere. Some of the little vehicles showed a makeshift destination sign behind the windshield. Others had no windshield or simply were known to their regular passengers. Among all this, the U.S. military convoys plowed along like elephants, herded by jeeps and weapons carriers.

Many of the long military truck convoys were hauling supplies and equipment from the growing gray fleet anchored out in Manila Bay, a fine large anchorage. Varieties of landing craft served as lighters. Little usable dock space was available. Many of these landing craft would simply nose straight in to shore, dropping their drive-off ramps to reveal loaded trucks with their engines rumbling. Everyone was still in a hurry. The locals also were all struggling to make a buck on this new system. All round, and at all hours, men were buying, selling, renting and/or stealing. These Filipinos and Chinese were first class entrepreneurs who had been hardened and trained during the harsh occupation. Now they preyed on us.

Looking further out into the western end of the harbor, I saw another great fleet, a dead one. There in serried ranks sat hundreds, perhaps thousands, of big and small seagoing vessels. Many had their main decks permanently awash. Most remained upright, their keels buried in the bottom muck. Some showed only their masts and funnels at high tide. American aircraft had surprised and killed the fleet at anchor with precision bombing. The ranks of low-lying vessels, some just deckhouses, bridges, funnels and masts in view, would never venture out to sea again.

As those first depot days wore on, I began to encounter more old friends and acquaintances. Some were from college days, others from Benning, several from units where I'd served in the States. A core group of Syracuse University classmates and confederates coalesced. We would share brief days together before being dispatched to our separate locations.

One evening I left the depot with a pair of new friends to visit one of the quickly established regimental officers' clubs. Such clubs now dotted the better residential neighborhoods that remained standing in Manila. This club was pretty typical: a small walled front garden was protected by an iron gate. This faced the street. Behind it, a stucco residence, single story, overhanging eaves, lots of vines and flowers. Inside, rooms converted into a dining area, a reading room, a large card room, then in the back a good-size bar with newly built booths along the outside walls. The sound level was high, but not raucous, the tone masculine.

My first surprise of the evening was finding a Syracuse University ROTC companion running the place. The lieutenant was duded up in pinks and full class-A attire, as behooved the club manager. I'd not seen him since OCS, but he had certainly landed butter-side up. He kept his eye on the blackjack and poker games while we visited a bit. He was a natural.

After this short catch-up, we visitors wandered through the house and into the bar, where I slid into a booth just inside the back door. Before the second round of drinks arrived, that door banged open and a very tall voice asked loudly, "Jensen, what the hell are you doing here?" I jumped up and twisted to see my closest friend from Syracuse, Bill Purdie, grinning down at me. He was sent to the 82nd Infantry when we graduated from OCS and I thought he was still in Europe, which he obviously was not.

Our friendship dated back to the early fall of 1940 when we were frosh at the Maxwell School at Syracuse University. He was dating a girl who graduated from Penn Yan Academy with me just that spring. While I was training and retraining troops in Dixieland, he had, as he put it, been the first American officer to walk across every bridge from France through Austria. His outfit was pulled out of Europe and sent via the States to be in the now-cancelled Honshu invasion. They had just arrived, having been at sea when Japan quit.

Several other friends from Benning, Syracuse, and various shared posts also turned up. We became a rolling reunion, our first and last get-together. We did a great deal of reminiscing, eating and drinking as we filled our waiting days.

One of our guys, by clever means never perfectly made clear to me, laid hands on a small Filipino sailboat. We learned we could keep it afloat if two passengers bailed steadily. We never did find time to haul it out and caulk the leaking seams of this vintage craft, but we found time daily to go out sailing. We wallowed along in the crisscrossing waves of the muddy Pasig River, repeatedly cursed by the officious operators of military landing craft. We knew our course was erratic because of the heavy chop, gusts of undependable wind, and the long, heavy boom of the sail, which slatted over our bowed heads. The tiller man steered a wobbly course between looming disasters.

We felt fortunate to a have arranged a dependable source of local beer from Manila's largest brewery along with some crushed ice to cool off its hot recycled bottles. I believe this big brewery was the first large industry to gain a post-war foothold on the market. The Manila and Back Rail Road was another, but we had already patronized that. We thoughtfully agreed that it was not really bad beer, but there had been no really bad beer anywhere. What was its name?

Ah yes, the name of this unforgettable malt beverage: "San Miguel." Most soldiers called it "Sam McGill," the latter name coming more easily upon the Anglo tongue. But the label on any booze was not of consequence. Many of the bottles had been recycled from occupation days. In those post-war days traditional American blended whiskies, like Three Feathers, Four Roses and Golden Wedding were daily distilled for bottling by almost every unit of any size. Consumer pricing by the entrepreneur was a bit lower if any empty bottle with cap and label intact could be traded in. After one or two shots these local distillations did taste pretty much as we remembered the professionally produced stateside blend.

This oriental whiskey was, of course, made from any available ingredients. Much depended upon the contents of mess hall scraps and scrapings, purloined sugar and bootlegged, peculiar yeasts. Processes were innovated, often requiring fermentation and boiling in GI cans or dubious vats no longer needed for warlike liquids, then misted into and dripped through coils of new or used copper tubing into the genuine labeled bottles. Any aging, regardless of the statements on those labels, normally took place while the bottle contents cooled. Some of these dubious brands we consumed in our tents, about ten months later.

We were celebrating the first Philippine Independence Day on July 4, 1946. An announcement had come down that there would be a large parade and many fireworks celebrating this great occasion in downtown Manila. We were free to attend and to join in the celebration, a new national holiday. I was on hand awaiting another reassignment, just killing time. Like many others, I decided I had had enough parades and would enjoy being farther away from the fireworks, explosives and sky-shooting so dear to indigenous personnel. We watched from our quarters. On this day I also discovered that Manila-made Southern Comfort was one brand which did not live up to the original formula, although the proof level was higher.

A few days after the Tarlac round-trip, everything changed for me. I received orders for my new unit. I was transferred to HQ AFWESPAC, Headquarters, American Forces, Western Pacific. Duties undefined at General MacArthur's headquarters in Manila (though He was now in Tokyo). This would be a real change from my unit experience as an enlisted man and a commissioned officer. I'd always been led and/or leading. This would be a staff function of some kind. I wondered what, and where, but the very change would be welcome after my last stateside duties. There I'd been engaged in retraining surplus air force non-coms into infantry jobs they did not want, mounting guard over pens of reluctant German prisoners, and drilling infantry basic graduates in the ways of antitank guns. Things were looking up. I packed my bags and reported to the new HQ. Then came the surprise.

Safe Hand Air Courier Service

When the jeep's driver deposited me outside Manila's temporary HQ AFWESPAC, evidenced by an office prefab building, I could only wonder where I would start my new staff assignment. A clerk had me dump my bags, and then pointed me down one of the long hallways. An open doorway at the end was labeled "Safe Hand Air Courier Service." Inside, a high counter separated me from a small room crowded by four desks, two chairs apiece, one swivel, the other straight armless, some maps and waste cans, and two persons. The nearer one was a short non-com standing behind the long counter. The other one displayed a gold oak leaf on his collar, some ribbons banked over his left shirt pocket. A major. Leaning back in his chair, he eyed me dispassionately.

"You Jensen? Let me see your orders. You are now a Safe Hand Air Courier. Got that?" He did not stand up so I did not salute, nor did he offer to shake my hand.

I simply responded properly, "Yessir, yessir, yes Sir!" It appeared that I would be going places. I had never heard of the organization before. Quickly and routinely, the major outlined the situation for his new pilgrim.

Pointing from his chair toward a big regional map of the Western Pacific ocean and the bits and pieces of land in and around it, he indicated with one sweep a long line of red arrows and small explosive dots rearing northward from Australia to Tokyo.

Scattered along the line were two dots in New Guinea, one each in Biak and Mindanao, then Manila, Takao, Okinawa and a smaller variety of side routes around the Philippines.

"General MacArthur's mail routes," he recited. "Safe Hand Couriers fly into every one of his command airports on one plane or another, every day. Our couriers all are commissioned officers, and we handle only designated official Safe Hand Mail under our personal care. Every Safe Hand office is a secure office guarded by our own people.

Every Safe Hand item is in a Safe Hand bag. Our couriers have landed right behind the attacking lines on the islands, but so far we have had only one serious casualty." He paused, said significantly, "One of our lieutenants was bitten by some dam' virus bug while screwing in some bushes." I responded by nodding my head vigorously.

Safe Hand Couriers flying the base leg into Australia were still creating another danger, less apparent. Some few of them were running private businesses which required assembling American cigarettes in cartons, bagging them and delivering them to individuals in Australia in trade for numerous quarts of kangaroo land whiskey, rum, gin and vodka to be brought up on the return flight. The proceeds were usable in establishing postwar businesses. This trade was slowing down, the commanders believed hopefully. I nodded my understanding, and the warning implicit in the orientation speech.

Simply, my job as a courier would be to pick up the Safe Hand Mail, sign for it, take it from our airport office and carry it to the correct plane, then fly with it to the designated airport and deliver it to the designated Safe Hand office and get a receipt. Sooner or later, I would return to my "Home" station and take a day or two off before my next flight. I was never to ask or tell what was contained in any bag, or think about it. Just get billing and receipts, signatures and dates.

"Got that?"

"Got it." My training was complete, and I had another new MOS. Next came the real surprise.

"You will be stationed at Hollandia, New Guinea, until further notice. You leave this morning." This time I saluted, did an about-face, and escaped in proper military protocol. From the front room, I followed the Safe Hand Air Courier scheduled to take the mail down to Zamboanga, Biak, Hollandia and Finschaven en route to Australia. At the edge of a long runway an army version of the old DC-3, a C-47, was coughing up fume blobs from its starboard engine. I threw my bags into the rear cargo hatch and clambered up a steep ladder behind the courier.

Inside, metal bucket seats resembling old-fashioned washbasins lined the walls, safety harnesses behind each one. Tiny oval plexi-windows like sealed portholes leaked in daylight through their maze of cracks and scratches. Any interior electric lights were off.

A few soldiers were already asleep in uncomfortable positions here and there along the sides. Others were holding up magazines and newspapers, squinting at them where the yellowish daylight made such reading possible. Not all of the large boxes and bags of stuff smelled bad there in the wide center aisle. Some were trapped under mesh cargo nets, others looked to be loose. Quite a bit of dried fish, I decided.

And some kind of swampy roots and poorly dried meat, evidently. This plane was general cargo for indigenous personnel as well as American troop units. We pulled the Safe Hand bags and my gear around our feet, and waited in silence.

"Fly low," grumbled my guide, not looking at me.

"Fly where?"

"No, fly low. Low down," he muttered. "These are all short hops today so this plane will fly at a thousand feet or so, not up high. It's cold up there even at the equator. Need warmer clothes for long flights. Safe, too, low."

I surreptitiously felt of the thick leather flap on my GI pistol holster, and fondled the weight of the old .45-caliber automatic dangling off my right hipbone. My thoughts veered way back to infantry basic training at Camp Wheeler, where a battle-proven cadre man told recruits, "The effective range of this model 1911 pistol is about fifteen feet, or as far as you can throw it."

Reassured, I next slumped into the seat until we slowly rumbled out onto the end of the runway, then accelerated, screaming at full throttle, bouncing a few times and oozing into the bright blue sky. The sky must have been blue; it looked blurry green through the porthole. Soon we leveled out, wheels already retracted, and lumbered off over the treetops and occasional muddy rivers and bays, headed for that port of tailless monkeys, Zamboanga.

So began my short career as an air courier. Well, an apprentice, at this point. We soared gracelessly down to a rough landing on their dirt strip. The cargo door slid back to let steamy air into the plane, which was already beginning to reach baking temperature. We hastily delivered, picked up, signed for, receipted, and performed the rest of the routine, hastening back to the dubious shelter of the aircraft. There we waited while required takeoff preparations were performed and checked off their respective lists, and we sweated ourselves wet. Passengers got off. Others got on and sat down. No tickets seemed to be needed. The door slammed, was latched and locked, and off we went again, to repeat the same procedure at the smaller Biak Island airstrip. Snoozing, smoking, saying little, we occasionally stared down through our tiny windows at the sea, which now rolled crossways beneath our broad wings. The port engine seemed to be pulsing, then eased back into a steady roar.

Below us a native vessel appeared, a catamaran or dhow, with a long, low lateen-rigged sail. It seemed to be coffee colored, as did the crew and passengers who were waving fists and long shining knives up at us. I'd have bet they were shouting, too, at U.S. liberators overhead.

"Dam' hotshot pilots try to blow over those Moro catamarans," explained my guide. "They get bored, especially the dam' Aussies. Big old engines create a big old draft. Tip 'em over, sometimes. Bastids shoot at the planes, but their old guns ain't that accurate. Flips say the Moros got gills, like fish, they swim so good." This encyclopedic entry reported, he subsided and dozed off. I thought and watched the water for more local craft.

Several hours later, after a stop at Biak Island's air base, we circled and descended to land at Hollandia's military airport. The field looked deserted. I had been expecting more: more runways, more jungle, more people around, more activity. This was simply a long dusty runway, no more.

A couple of GIs strolled out to meet us as the pilot swung the C-47 clumsily around on the grass ramp, ready to take off again. The pair was half of the Safe Hand station's staff, identifiable as soldiers mostly because they were both obviously white. And because they acted as if they'd been anticipating our plane's arrival. Both wore cut-off khaki shorts and T-shirts with pictures on the front. The shorter one wore flip-flops, shower slippers. The taller one was in dust-covered brown army dress shoes, though he was sockless.

Who were these geeks? I couldn't tell. Neither wore a name tag nor any sign of rank. They looked happy and relaxed, almost as if they were civilians back home. I handed down my two bags, plus two Safe Hand Mail bags tagged "Hollandia," and jumped out the door to shake hands. The tall one was a tech sergeant who said, "Call me Swanny." He would become my close companion before I learned Swanson's complete name. The short one, wearing a grease-stained outfit, was a T-corporal who serviced the strip's freestanding bank of truck-sized diesel generators. Just one of these was loafing at idle, providing effortlessly all the power this outfit was likely to need for lights and radio. Only its deep, growling hum broke the background silence around us. A light breeze stirred the weedy grass and the dangling leaves of a few nearby trees, whipping an occasional tiny dust devil across the dirt.

I considered what I observed. This looked like a good place for a small-town boy to lay low until time to go home. So it proved for a few unbelievable months.

We hopped into a topless jeep for a ride of several hundred feet to the large olive drab Quonset hut that was the Safe Hand office. Though the small building stood alone and lonely, around it several army trucks were parked — or rather, left — in casual places. It looked like a disordered company motor pool, and I asked if there were other troops about. The bumper-painted insignia identified infantry, signal corps, engineer, cavalry and other units. Then I learned these were all our vehicles, at least four or five for each of us, and that neither enlisted drivers nor any military driver's license was even thought of. "Just take it and gas it up over there," said Swanny, pointing at some massive horizontal fuel tanks. "We keep the oil in the office now."

We went in the screen door which was the only door, to find a first lieutenant doing paperwork about his points, and a handsome Negro who sat reading personal mail. The latter man was weirdly attired for a soldier, I had to notice. Slender and muscular, he sported a very tight lemon yellow T-shirt with both sleeves rolled high, his cigarettes and a Zippo lighter tucked in the left cuff. His trousers were blue navy work jeans, bleached nearly white and equally tight. He wore high-topped white sneakers with blue laces. And shoved back on his curly hair was a bleached-denim boonie hat, its brim turned down all the way around.

After introductions, the unlikely-attired corporal, for that was his rank, clued me in. "Lootenant, you want to go down to the lake villages, we can go anytime. These people like me, specially the women." He grinned at me. And when I did have to go to the Sentenai Lake villages for a good but different reason, he became a knowledgeable and helpful guide. (Of this more later). He was from some Midwestern city, but said he planned to come back here after the war. He must have looked like a god to the little Micronesian tribal people, for they were intensely black, powerfully short, covered with warty scars and markings, and as nearly naked as they were ignorant of civilized ways.

I now knew that Hollandia was not exactly here. Hollandia was 25 or 30 miles down The Million Dollar Highway to our southeast. This aptly named scenic route had been bulldozed out of hillsides laden with gold-bearing soil in order to connect the port and this new airfield. It took only a day or two — a week, some said — to complete. I never found any gold myself. Anyone stopping to prospect ran the risk of being shot by remnant snipers who refused to believe the war was over. The dirt road was still in decent condition, though the construction crews were long gone on their road to Tokyo. Motor traffic was limited, to say the least, without any rush hours.

Several factors contributed to this traffic control. Only a few scattered special-purpose troop units remained. The U.S. was not occupying this northwest segment of New Guinea to police it. The troops were mostly engineers and signal corps, I think, plus a few Australians near us, and of course the U.S. Navy people down at the port of Hollandia, with their warehouses full of stores, beer, and freezers. We were out at the end of the winding trail. No one seemed to need to come visiting much.

When I did go in to Hollandia, I learned another good reason why people did not casually drive the lower end of the highway. Nearer the coast, the road passed through many large plantations, a stretch of ten miles or so. The plantation owners still were Dutch, for this had been Dutch New Guinea. The managers and foremen were Indonesians. The workers were, largely, Melanesians, taller and lighter than the local Micronesian primitives who had lived here all history and before.

Now that the Japanese occupation troops had been cleared out, the three darker-skinned groups were in revolt against their Dutch proprietors. They also were in a three-way fight among themselves. Being neutral non-combatants, we Americans flew large U.S. flags on our trucks, and we did not stop to chat. We'd hear occasional sniping, or a burst of automatic fire near the road somewhere. Once in a while a stray shot would crack and whistle overhead, let loose by some unbeliever. Only the local units' courier trucks usually came out as far as our airstrip.

As I write in 2003, the Dutch are long gone; the former territory appears on newer maps as West Irian Jaya. Hollandia's name has been changed to Jayapura. And the winners are....

My Free Vacation on a Tropical Island

"People pay thousands of dollars for a vacation trip like this" was a popular army saying whenever we were going into a new assignment. The fitting response was a laconic "Yeah!" This isolated Safe Hand courier station outside Hollandia, though, did prove to be an exception for me. Of course, there were a few spots....

My first afternoon at Sentenai Air Strip, after the daily hour of rain had freshened the air, the lieutenant-about-to-leave took me up to officers' quarters. Unlike any other post I'd seen or heard about, the area consisted of a row of small bungalows shaded by tall trees, backed up to a deep, forested gully. The tinkling of a small stream came from the quiet depths.

Overwhelmed, I turned to my new base commander, about to ask questions. The quarters looked like a high-priced AAA auto court on Route 66, I commented. He forestalled me, saying "These were the senior officers' quarters for General MacArthur's Hollandia headquarters staff... bird colonels and brigadier generals or higher brass. Now they're all vacant. You take the one next to mine." Whereupon he went inside to take a nap while I settled in.

Obeying orders, I pulled open a real screen door and walked into the two-room cabin. Each room had an iron cot with a mattress, wooden bureau, table desk, and two chairs. The screened windows had shutters but no glass, local style. I pushed open the shutters to air out the slight stuffiness. The view was all natural, no parade ground anywhere. No people sounds, just some rustling and squawking overlay the stream's murmuring.

I quickly unpacked, hanging my winter uniforms, trench coat and field jacket in the open closet area, polished shoes and spare boots aligned beneath. Khakis I hung next, mostly from force of habit. The rest I folded into the bureau drawers or arranged neatly on bureau and tabletops. Well, I thought, I won't need most of this until my orders come for the States. All organized and secure. I lay down on the cot and dozed while waiting for my jeep ride back to the office. "Sabbatical leave..." I remember thinking. After a few cold beers at the Safe Hand office, we had a casual supper of sandwiches and canned stuff; then coffee, of course, accompanied by views of a magnificent sunset and the quick appearance of the Southern Cross and a few other stars in the darkening sky. My new companions in informality regaled me with stories about The General's luxurious headquarters above us on the mountain. The giant residence, headquarters, and facilities had been built in jig-time before MacArthur's arrival.

The Commanding General, however, was in a great hurry, and stayed there only briefly or not at all during his prophesied Return to The Philippines campaign. Now it stood abandoned, as was the natural swimming pool created in a rushing stream nearby. The Safe Hand crew spent midday at this pool between morning and afternoon flights, often leaving only one member at the office to handle any rush of local business. I never did see anyone else up there. The water was chilly, the sun agreeably hot.

Next morning we breakfasted at the Australian encampment a few miles down the road toward Hollandia. I think this was mostly as an indoctrination for me. Safe Hand personnel were attached to the Aussie unit for rations and quarters, though we mostly kept to ourselves. We drew fresh rations and some staples to cook at our place, and slept at the field. At this meal, I discovered one motivation for this. Breakfast was cold leftover spaghetti in tomato sauce, with bread, jam, and hot tea. The only other morning I appeared there for breakfast, the entrée was cold stewed tomatoes.

We carried back a supply of fresh-frozen chickens, fresh beef, butter, eggs, and powdered eggs, dry milk and a number of one-gallon cans containing cooked ham, turkey, and chicken, plus assorted condiments and a supply of both flour and sugar. With this and certain arrangements to have fresh U.S. Army bread flown down from Biak, and coffee and other beverages north from Australia in custody of our couriers, we toughed it out. Every day was a cookout, a steak fry or a chicken fry, ham and eggs, toast, and so on. We were a little light on fresh vegetables, but always had a stem of bananas and lots of cooking plantains from our native neighbors. Usually we feasted after the second plane had left.

After dark, we repaired to the office to read or play cards by electric light and to talk about home. At bedtime, we two officers would drive up to our private cabins in our own jeeps, parking them with their headlights illuminating the buildings until we could light the lanterns inside. This did seem unreal, but we slept soundly, lulled by the night noises and the deep darkness of our surroundings.

The evening view was disturbingly different a week later. Our screen doors were hanging open. The place had been ransacked. Our clothes and belongings were gone except for odds and ends scattered about. Papers and some socks littered a trail broken through the weeds into the black silence of our gully.

"I guess now the natives have clothes," I said foolishly. My associate was busy cussing. "I wonder what they'll do with the woolen uniforms," I muttered, though not very loudly.

We trucked the cots and mattresses down to our headquarters to sleep overnight, though we might just have safely slept in the burglarized cabins. The next day we moved our remaining gear into the big back room of the Quonset hut and requisitioned some new clothing out of Biak. We also planned a trip down to that nearest lake village in search of any clothes which might fit us and have our names on them.

We took the colorful corporal with us as our guide and convincer. He said he was well acquainted with those folks at the lake.

Negotiating a rough track fashioned more for feet than wheels, we drove down to the lakefront clearing behind the clump of houses. Even as a kid who grew up on a lakefront I'd never seen anything quite like this.

I stared out a dozen or so good-sized dwellings perched high on randomly driven posts out in the shallows of this bay. Some posts were straight tree trunks; others looked more like branches, with bends, angles, and stubs of broken limbs. Wood smoke drifted up through the low-hanging fronds of thatching, adding the smells of drying fish to a lower-level stink. The overhanging roofs hung low, darkening the interiors where wide window openings let the breezes through. No one moved on the porches or walkways between the homes. Beneath, some large and small dugout canoes were tethered to posts like family cars parked in the driveway. Occasionally, movement was apparent inside.

We carefully trod out on a single plank walkway that led from the beach. Loose boards overlapped at the ends as the bridge zigzagged between posts. Everyone had to know we were coming. The planks rattled and bent beneath our weight, and the posts seemed shaky. But as we stooped to enter, our corporal in the lead, nobody looked at us.

I peered quickly around, considering an unlikely ambush, but there was no place to hide. The hut walls were narrow slats, probably lake-edge reeds. The floor was slatted, bamboo in the round, and just fine for bare feet. Some five feet below, the lake surface undulated and riffled in patterns. Several open squares pierced the deck, without coverings or guardrails. A two-foot square opening near the center provided the water supply by means of a nearby bucket and rope. In a corner was the garbage disposal and toilet opening. Near the front door, a handy three-foot square opening yawned over the canoes in the garage. Hastily scanned, this was a picture of primitive communal living.

This all-purpose room was quite smoky, and the aroma of fish prevailed at this time. A smoldering fire in a sand box on the floor was drying a rack full of gutted and filleted fish. This added little to the ambiance, but probably served also as a pilot light for hotter cooking fires. A woman squatted on her heels next to the firebox, just watching. She was not wearing any of our clothes.

The woman and a silent man seemed ageless, like small children grown old. They were not dwarfs, but short and quite thin, with bushy hair and weathered walnut skin, dark eyes their only moving parts. Also strangely silent and still were several kids of assorted ages who gathered near the farthest wall to observe us. The children were naked, which seemed very appropriate for the place and temperatures. The adults were heavily scarred in ceremonial patterns, though their youngsters bore mostly facial markings. Everybody looked innocent.

All this consumed a minute or two. Our lieutenant leader then stepped toward the adults and spoke to them in English, gesturing and with expression, quite loudly and very, simply, slowly. His audience spoke only their tribal language, so his words probably were as effective as would have been Dutch, Spanish, or one of the Malay tongues; but it was all we had available and would have to do.

"We have been robbed. We demand our clothes and belongings which were stolen from our homes. We believe you people have them. Give them back now." And so on.

The grownups looked at us blankly, though the kids chattered among themselves like a Greek chorus. After several minutes, the man looked at the woman, who said a few words in the native language. Our boss looey turned inquiringly to the corporal for a translation. The corporal shook his head and shrugged, showing his hands: his personal acquaintanceship with locals here had not been based on much verbal communication. The lieutenant wiggled his right thumb and scowled. The corporal swung into a long pantomime of explanation, ending with a vigorous threat that we would immediately search the place. The woman talked to the man, who frowned, then waved permissively to us. I had a feeling these families had been searched before.

We quickly looked through their house as the family watched, but found nothing. We repeated our procedure in the other village homes, turning up some souvenirs from the contending armies, but nothing of ours. A search along the gully trails the next day turned up my trench coat and a few other pieces of winter clothing lost or tossed away by the daylight raiders. The culprits were never found, and we thought had not come from that nearest village. The hunt was over.

"It's not worth any more time," said Swanson. "Almost everything belonged to the army anyway." We went back to our daily routine. I found many advantages to bunking in the office Quonset with its electric light and tin roof that rattled in the afternoon rainstorms.

The poured concrete floor of the Quonset was cool and bugless. My cot would shake and travel along that floor in our near-daily minor earthquakes. At first it was surprising to feel the shudders as the iron feet chattered around on the floor, but the small tremors did us no damage and caused no fears.

Soon the points-happy lieutenant flew off toward Manila on his way home, and the Tec Two also left on orders. I was left in command of the Hollandia SACS station, just three of us at quiet Sentenai Strip. This amounted to an honorary position. We all took turns at handling incoming and outgoing mail, and usually were all present for the flights. Mostly we read, wrote, swam and prepared meals, with plenty of nap-time. This was indeed light duty.

One day a skinny Melanesian kid showed up. He spoke a few words of Army, and quickly fitted himself into our camp life. His quick enthusiasm and his taking over the sweeping and wood-gathering chores combined to amuse us, as did his successful use of pidgin language. He was always informing me what things were.

"Sen terre," he'd say slowly, holding up a GI flashlight. "Sen terre." Then he'd point to the headlights on a jeep: "Auto Senterre." "Auto Senterre." This was one of his first lessons and I still remember it. Soon I became fluent in approximately twenty words of some language.

When Sam, as we named him, appeared before us, he wore a pair of ragged khaki shorts and a sleeveless white undershirt long enough to cover them. He was hatless, though his black hair had been chopped fairly short. He stood about five feet tall in his large bare feet. I guessed he might be twelve years old. In his leather belt he wore a scabbard containing a combat knife, in his left hand carried a small bow and a handful of featherless arrows.

Once we accepted him, Sam would come and go, apparently to his parents' village somewhere nearby. He'd bring fruit, and next time we'd send off surplus food and interesting stuff from our supply. In camp, he slept in one of the parked trucks.

One morning I found Sam working on some new arrows, a pile of slender reed stems next to him as he sat in the dirt. He was nursing a tiny fire of twigs over which he would straighten the three-foot stems. After sighting along the length to locate a crooked area, he would mark the spot with a thumb, then lean forward to heat that part over the fire until he could straighten it. This he did by pulling the heated arrow up between his toes. He repeated this slow process until the shaft was all straight. Finally he rotated the reed over the fire to harden both ends.

I was interested in these arrows, which were not notched or pointed. The short ironwood bow used a flat strip of reed for a bowstring. Sam centered the back end of the arrow against the string with his callused thumb and forefinger. The hardened tip at the front end was a shock weapon for knocking over small game at close range, as he demonstrated to me. "Birds," he signed, "Small Animals. Fish." I admired his outfit and his skill.

A few days later Sam brought me a black wood adult-size bow and three five-foot arrows as a gift. The arrows had varied points. Two were long thin ironwood pieces, sharpened and notched points inserted into the thick reed shafts and bound with fibers. The third was a fish spear, with a cluster of five or six long points made into a cup shape, of the heavy black wood. All arrows were decorated with wood burning. These were not feathered or fletched , apparently depending on the force of the bow to drive them straight in flight. This kit became my only souvenir when I left Hollandia.

The days drifted along with occasional high spots. One morning we heard men's voices chanting. We jumped into a jeep and drove to the other end of the strip, where we found about twenty Negritos skidding a big new dugout toward Sentenai Lake. Most of the stocky little black men were tugging on ropes, a few pushing and guiding the massive tree trunk toward a beach. They stopped work as we pulled up alongside their hollowed-out log.

The canoe would be taken off to some village across the wide lake, they pointed. The tribesmen had traveled several miles to the tall jungle to pick the right tree. Once the trunk had been felled, they had burned and adzed it to rough shape. Finally they had hollowed out the inside with simple hand tools before dragging it cross-country toward home.

We howdied with signs and smiles, then went over to admire their big project. Their leader joined us. He was an older man, nearly five feet tall, who had the most-decorated skin of all. He pointed down toward the lake a good half-mile away. He was hitching a ride. We tethered the bow of their canoe to the jeep bumper and were off, with most of the natives sitting inside the boat, and a few jogging alongside to steady it on its course. At lakeside, we unhitched, shook hands all round, and departed with lots of grinning and laughing.

One afternoon I was minding the shop while the others were up on the mountain swimming. It was a matter of whiling the time between flights, so I was alone in the Safe Hand office Quonset. Unexpectedly, a large olive drab command car pulled up dustily out front. It bore a huge American flag staffed on the front bumper, not the routine smaller ensign displayed to ease the way of VIPs and high-ranking officers. An important courier, thought I.

I could see two khaki-clad non-coms sitting stiffly in the front seats as the dust settled. They remained silent and vigilant as a well dressed major with a visored and eagled cap climbed down from the rear seat. He had been sharing it with what looked like a large wooden ammo box. Not at all the usual casual junior officer was this man.

I went to the counter as he strode into the Quonset office, looking about as if he expected to see more troops on guard, or some, at least. He halted some two feet from the high counter and barked.

"Lieutenant!"

"Yes Sir," I answered, secure in my defilade position. "Do you have Safe Hand Mail to go?"

"You're damned right. I've got a million dollars in gold out there you need to Safe Hand out today, in that big box! Sign this chit." With that announcement he pulled from his shiny briefcase an original and several carbon copies of a manifest, tossing them onto my counter. "Now you are responsible."

Breathing deep, I gathered my wits, I left the papers right there, without my fingerprints.

"I'm sorry, Sir, the Safe Hand Air Courier Service carries only bags and cartons of SACS mail. We are not responsible for contents. In fact I am not supposed to know the contents of any parcel which crosses that counter. Orders, sir. I'm sure you can see how that would be."

"No," he said, and stood there. I explained twice more in the same words.

Without thanking me, he grabbed up the manifests, jabbed them into his case, and stormed back to the command car. It roared off, circling on the dirt and disappearing down the roadway toward Hollandia.

I never learned where he came from or where he was trying to send his box. Funny, all he had to do was follow the rules.

Christmas week I received orders to close down our Hollandia SACS station. This southern route had served its purpose. We picked up and packed up our personal stuff and the basic Safe Hand reports, burning piles of accumulated paper. We would abandon vehicles and buildings in place, this being cheaper than shipping things elsewhere to be junked. Most of the moveable equipment had already been written off by previous "owners." It was here, but did not exist.

Our small native handyman said his father would like to have the tools and the canned foods we were leaving behind, so we loaded a couple of our "deuce and a half" cargo trucks and drove them down to a stream crossing about three miles off. There we left them, and one jeep, beside a broad, shallow stream flowing down from the high mountains.

As the sound of the engines died for that last time, a small dugout slipped down from the forested valley. Poling it was a tall Melanesian who had come to collect his son. They pushed off their boat and awaited our departure, smiling and occasionally waving. We went back to the strip where the generator too was silent, and boarded the afternoon C-47 courier plane for Zamboanga and Manila.

On that low, slow flight, I wondered where, and if, I would be flying SACS bags next. Were the local inter-island routes around the Philippines still functioning? How many more experienced couriers were still available? My orders did not transfer me to any other unit. Of one thing I was pretty sure: it was the end of my free vacation.

Down the Runway

Just a few days after my return to Manila Base from Hollandia, I stood waiting at foggy daylight to once again board a flight with Safe Hand Air Courier bags. Even at sea level and near the Equator, I felt chilled and damp in Manila. Puffing on a smoke, I considered the positive, which had been assignment to fly as a courier, and the negative, that I would not fly on a U.S. Air Force plane today. I'd be riding with the new Philippine Air Force. This meant the pilots and crew would be new, too, an unknown quantity. I shivered as I stripped the butt and ground out the smoldering tobacco remnants. The mist was lifting.

Today's courier trip should be a milk run, from Manila to Manila by way of three of the larger islands, Mindoro, Panay, and Leyte, then back up Luzon to home base.

I carried several small bags of Safe Hand Mail for the first two stops and three large heavy bags addressed to the Finance

Officer at Leyte's Tacloban City headquarters. A half-million freshly printed Filipino peso bills were being sent out for use in that area's cash-starved economy. I was not supposed to know or reveal the contents of these bags, of course. I was glad to be officially responsible only for the Safe Hand bags, which were all I'd signed for.

When the three-man crew strolled out toward the plane, I was shocked. I thought of uniformed Boy Scouts who should not be smoking cigarettes and sipping hot coffee. The taller pilot wore his cap with a 50-mission crush; the shorter had his squared off and pulled down to eyebrow level. The pilot and the co-pilot, I'd bet money. A scrawny non-com in wrinkled greens, wearing an overseas cap raked over one ear, must be the crew chief. What was I getting into?

"Too short, too thin, too happy, and too young" to fly this big old cargo plane, I murmured. The clumsy C-47 had proud new markings, but I could see where they had painted over the USAF's white stars on the wings and fuselage. I became more wakeful as we readied for departure and nobody else came out from the office.

Ours would be a hop-skip-and jump trip today, short legs of a hundred or 150 miles, and much of it over forested land or at least near beaches. I'd checked the chart, since this was new territory for me. I might as well get comfortable for now.

I dragged the bags up to the front of the cargo compartment, choosing my favorite spot where I could have the most comfortable ride and look out over the port engine nacelle as we flew low over the network of islands and sea. I eased back in one of the aluminum washbasin seats and propped my nearly new kangaroo jump boots against the cover of a large mahogany casket in the aisle. A local general was being shipped home to Iloilo, our Panay stop, for burial. The rest of this plane was piled with miscellaneous boxes, bags, and bundles. Two more native men in cotton shirts and khaki shorts came up the ladder and sat way in the back. They were talking together. I considered that the war had now been over for four months, so why worry? My thoughts were jumping around.

Suddenly the starboard engine kicked over a few times, paused, and burst into its roar, then throttled down to an idle rumbling. The port engine required a couple of love pats from the crew chief before it would start but then ran up to speed and back to idle, barking and coughing before it smoothed out. Port engines always left me nervous.

I watched as the crew chief darted under my wing to snatch out the wheel chocks, and turned back as he boarded and pulled the cargo door shut to latch it. He quickly worked his way forward, shoving freight boxes and bags about to fill holes, eventually disappearing into the forward crew compartment, slamming the door behind him. We lumbered over to the metal runway and swung into takeoff position. The pilot set the brakes, and ran both engines up until the brakes squealed and the aircraft shuddered all over. When he finished this final test, he reduced throttle for a moment, then took us off, on the Road to Mindoro.

Our initial bearing took us very low over the great sunken Jap shipping fleet sticking out of Manila Harbor. Was it my imagination, or was that port engine running slower than the other one? I thought back to my first ride, en route to New Guinea, and the courier officer's growling commentary: "Low. Fly low. Low is safer...." Just then the engine speeded up and I relaxed again.

We soon dropped down onto the end of the long dirt strip that was Mindoro's only airfield, bouncing up and down two or three times on each wheel as we felt the brakes being pumped. Nothing collapsed, so it was a landing. I carried the Mindoro SACS bag to the cargo door as it was opened, and peered out as I awaited a pickup by the locals. The scene reminded me of Sentenai Lake airstrip on a miniature scale. A few Quonsets and temporary buildings, some big fuel tanks, a small fueling truck and a ratty-looking old hometown fire engine with its ladders missing. Several small brown men in army uniforms lounged around, but no one came to board the plane. Business was slow indeed here. A few packages off and on, then we'd head for Iloilo.

The crew chief was the only person who got off the plane. As he started his pre-flight visual walk-around, he began on my side. He stretched up to pull a strip of loose metal off the port engine. After waving it at the pilot above and grinning, he flung it out into the weeds. It didn't look like a working part. He dodged under the fuselage to continue his rounds, tapping on the landing gear struts and tires right below my feet. He closed up the back, and disappeared into the front office without a word to us passengers. I rearranged my bags and waited with pre-takeoff concentration.

Our pilot swung the bird around, and we rushed off down the strip, slowly gaining speed, lifting, rocking, swaying and bumping in sharp little wind gusts. I thought it felt like a pretty typical takeoff. It wasn't.

The next thing I knew, I was regaining consciousness, flat on my back, squeezed between the general's casket and the pilot compartment wall. All around was a red glare full of roaring burning noise, stinking gray smoke, and fear.

"I'm all alone," was my first thought as I struggled to roll over and to shove junk away from my narrow sanctuary. I crouched on hands and knees just below the harsh smoke, and tried to see back, but there was no light there. The port engine had torn off and was jamming the only exit door. Flames were shooting up through the deck, and I could see one tire burning fiercely in a pool of fuel. I'd never get into the pilot compartment before the cabin was engulfed, if there was a front still on the fuselage.

Without consciously making a decision, I pulled my .45-caliber automatic out of my new shoulder holster and shot most of the plexiglass out of the nearest window. I can't remember hearing the shots, even now. Pounding the edge fragments away I emptied the magazine. I made that little porthole as big as possible as fast as possible, and contorted my body to squeeze through headfirst. If I did not fear that the opening would prove too small, it was because I was struggling so hard. Within a minute I fell onto the top of the left wing, which was being licked along its edges by the fire. I limped, gasping, to the tip, where I flew gracelessly to the dirt, making a running landing as something blew up behind me.

As I staggered away, coughing and hacking up the noxious fumes, the screams started in the rear of the burning plane. I still awaken to them from time to time, nearly sixty years later. I visualize the shrunken black crisps of two bodies I saw the next morning, where they had toppled from the tail washroom into the charred shadow of the C-47. The men had blundered into the windowless toilet as they attempted to find a way out.

I seldom think of the half-million pesos. No one ever asked me about them when I reported in Manila to be briefed out. Statistically, it was not a bad wreck. Three dead, including the now-cremated general, and four survivors — the entire crew plus one U.S. Army lieutenant. The C-47 had long-ago been written off.

An order wired from SACS AFWESPAC directed me to return there by first available transportation. Another courier plane would be along in two days. This routed me all around the islands to get back to Manila, and it would also be a Philippine Air Force plane.

Remembering again about the war being over, I hitched a ride down to the little fishing port on the bay and found a low, slow passage on an army FS boat carrying general cargo inter-island. I spent much time in the bow, watching sunlight flicker across wave tops. I felt safe once again on the wide China Sea, but I did not smoke.

<u>Some Strange Enough Voyages</u>

Shortly after landing from the FS boat at Manila, I requested a transfer to some other, non-flying, assignment. Perhaps in part because of the rawness in my voice, and the lingering fumes of aircraft fuel whenever I exhaled or had a coughing attack, personnel officers found a new and very different line of work for me.

"Okay, Jensen, you're going to sea. You're transferred immediately to the troop unit handling passengers aboard the Herman S. Snavely. It's a Liberty Ship. You're now the Special Services Officer." The captain handed me my orders without further information. I wondered if I'd be running bingo games or pool tables, or organizing games and dances and the daily ship's pool. Whatever, it would be a new experience.

I saluted and went back to barracks to pack up for pickup next morning. Deciding to look at the bright side, I repeated my two mantras: "I can't fly, but I can swim," and "Remember, Al, the war is over."

A jeep took me to a wharf on the busy waterfront, and there at the pier sat a large and clumsy-looking ship, a Liberty looming above me. Its single large funnel had a big flat cap brimming its top, and the gangplank ran straight up a good two stories from the rough wooden dock where I stood. I reared back to look at the Herman S. Snavely, one of 2,700 Liberty Ships whipped out to carry cargo, mostly, but alternatively troops. This was the design which had caused FDR to exclaim: "What a dreadful-looking object!" when he first saw the drawings back in 1941.

Let me pause to inject a bit of background here, for this was the first of two similar vessels on which I served during the next few months. "The Liberty Fleet," as U.S. Admiral Land euphemistically named it, was based on an 1879 cargo vessel design the English had been using, with few modifications, for sixty years. Cheap and easy to build and to operate, these ships had done their job effectively when the time factor was not important, so there'd been no reason to improve the slow cargo ships. More than 400 feet long, with a beam of nearly 58 feet, the tubby ship had a single big propeller driven by a vertical reciprocating steam engine. The large, simple engine was powered by two steam boilers, coal-fired still as in the old days. The Brits had come to the U.S. in 1940 bearing a slightly changed version of the plans which they called the Ocean class. They needed a huge fleet, quick and expendable, and only the U.S. had the workforce and capacity to build that fleet in time.

The new version called for equipping the hulls with an oil-fired engine, but apparently all the details were left up to the Americans. The Ocean class, and its big sister, the Liberty class of U.S. ships were built under the order to build ships more rapidly than the German U-boats could sink them. Each ship would be successful if it completed a single voyage. Our country's solution was a system radically different from the British routine of cutting, fitting, and riveting hulls together piece by piece in traditional shipyards. All construction was changed.

Welding had been perfected only in the 1930's, so now the new ships were welded, not riveted. Prefabrication on and off-site took on a bigger and bigger role. All was simplified and expedited as Henry Kaiser and a group known as "The Six Companies," all non-shipbuilding firms, took on the task. They used yards located from Maine to Oregon, some old, but mostly brand-new, and modified as they learned. A cruiser stern, a raked bow, soon the ships were being launched on a 40-day timetable from keel-laying to launch.

Like the Snavely, all the Liberties were 57 feet 8 inches beam width, 441 feet 6 inches long at the waterline, with 27 feet, 8½ inches draft, and five holds rated for 9,000 tons of cargo each. The triple-expansion steam engine developing 2,500 horsepower turned the huge propeller to enable a top speed of eleven knots, enough for slow convoy travel. Though designed for the choppy, stormy North Atlantic lifeline, these ships proliferated and soon were being used all around the world. Despite the predictions, only 200 were sunk during World War II service.

Although manned and operated by the Merchant Marine, each armed Liberty carried a Navy gun crew which handled two cannons, one three-inch forward and one five-inch aft, plus eight quick-firing 20mm guns in lightly-armored gun tubs. Ours still had the guns, but the Navy crews were gone.

My ship had been built on the West Coast in the spring of 1943, and fitted out as a troopship sometime later, probably for the Honshu invasion. If the basic design was an antique, the troop facilities were primitive indeed. All of the stairs (called ladders, of course) leading up from the troop compartments to the open deck were built like the outside steps my dad had built from our lakeside house up the bank to the state road. They were open-faced, strictly raw wood carpentry, with wooden railings on each side. The toilet facilities were true outhouses. They were racked along the railing, set atop the rail to be reached by a short flight of steps at each end, about twenty oval seats in each building. They looked like rows of chicken houses from the deck viewpoint, and quite dangerous from where I was down on the dock. I could not imagine using one in high seas. With no kitchen facilities, I supposed troops would have used field kitchens or eaten C or K rations, had our passengers been troops.

Expecting I would learn more eventually, I climbed the gangplank and reported to the troop commander. He was a shortish, squarish Transportation Corps captain who had been a railroad man on the Pennsy Line and a reservist in an army RR company. I thought him quite elderly, in his late 'thirties at least, with civilian-styled gray hair and a ruddy complexion. He genially introduced me to the other two team members, both first lieutenants, both named John, and both from his railroad outfit. Here we were, all sea transport specialists, just like that.

I quickly learned that my newest Military Occupational Specialty Number meant only that I was the most junior member of a small team which would supervise, manage and care for passengers. We were in the business of ferrying people back home, mostly. I learned that thousands of indigenous personnel had been moved around by their Japanese conquerors, uprooted from their homes and families and carried off to other countries to work or be jailed. This was a way of removing troublemakers and dissidents, preventing groups from forming.

We were a small factor in a large effort to take these populations back home quickly. We would take this load of Chinese back to the mainland at Amoy, and there pick up a bunch of Formosans to carry across the Strait of Formosa to their native island at Takao. At that stop we'd offload the Formosans, who were a blend of

Chinese/Japanese and thus foreigners to both. The final leg back to Manila, we'd be filled up with a variety of Filipino residents who had been forcibly taken to Formosa to work.

I was at last a working cog in a vast humanitarian effort, the sort of thing I had dreamed of back in high school before this war. It felt good. Though I knew nothing of the other, larger efforts that were now underway, it would be much better than having to kill people in large numbers — the purpose for which I assumed I'd been shipped out here.

This first voyage taught me a lot about our role as supercargo officers (for lack of a better title) and the intricate politics and bureaucratic bumbling which prevailed in our transactions with all involved: our bosses, the merchant marine captain, self-appointed group leaders and officially designated group leaders, and local officials, not to mention the senders and receivers of these poor displaced people. This herd of human cargo was not all friendly, not all grateful, and not one uniform mass but rather clusters of down beaten, angry and resentful people who did not necessarily believe life would ever get better.

We'd be carrying 900 or so mainland Chinese men, women, and children across the China Sea to Amoy. Dropping them off at this city of 300,000 was our final service to them. The trip would last four or five days, ending in the broad estuary at the mouth of the Amoy River after passing the little guardian islands of Matsu and Quemoy some fifteen miles offshore. The autocratic director of the movement, their official sponsor, was a rich Manila merchant, himself an overseas Chinese. When I arrived, he was already ensconced in the skipper's cabin, where he remained throughout the voyage. He departed as soon as we anchored, accompanied by many retainers and numerous containers. The rumor persisted that he had personal business that would enrich him further. It was not a problem for us.

Our work started with the help of translators from the traveling group, checking off Chinese names on the mimeographed manifest. This process was slowed by frequent loud discussions as we separated men and older boys from women and young children at the head of the gangplank. The men went aft to the two big holds behind the superstructure, and the kids with the women shared three holds forward. I wondered how many people there really were aboard, whether they were as named, if the names were male or female gender; but we got them aboard without fights.

The ship was not set up for mixed groups. I'm sure the designers thought only of organized and disciplined soldiers, not of a family cruise ship in foreign climes. Having been bullied and mistreated by the Japanese, these people were all afraid. They suspected every order, mistrusted every direction. Since their small group leaders relied on arm waving and shouting rather than persuasion or explanation, they had good reason to fear us. In the end, they went, and disappeared down the wooden steps into the designated holds amid a babble of excited voices.

The day's loading tapered off and stopped as the sun dropped out of sight beyond Corregidor. Going to dinner was a relief and comfort. We four ate in the officers' mess, located in the main deck superstructure with portholes facing the bow. These were open to catch any breeze. What a benefit! We were served by stewards, the food was as good as any American diner's, and there was even a mimeographed daily menu, complete with entrees and desserts. Well, only a few, but at least we had choices. Of all these meals, I remember most fondly the breakfast, with real eggs, and hot pancakes, ham or bacon, fresh rolls. Ahhhh....

It was at mess that I finally met most of the ship's officers at least once. Three remain memorable. Although I'd never tell him so, the skipper made me think of Count Felix von Luckner, "The Sea Devil." I'd seen photos of the famous German, captain of a shipping raider. This man, of only average stature, carried himself like a banty rooster. He was ever alert. His eyes, though sky blue, seemed never sunny. Smiles he clipped short, as he did his answers to questions or comments. He had been a lifetime at sea, and a long time in war.

The first mate could have been a Norwegian bachelor farmer. He was gangly but not awkward, with a long cheerful face as weather-tanned as that of any Midwestern outdoorsman. His soft voice and liquid syllables made me think of neighbors back home. I thought him very friendly, in spite of the scarred knuckles on his big, heavy hands.

The chief engineer I seldom saw except at one meal daily and later ashore under very different circumstances. He was big boned, with a large balding head. He wore his black-visored cap tipped back at all times. His manner of constantly nodding and swerving his head enlarged his presence whether he spoke or listened. He'd gone to sea from New Jersey as a stoker, and worked his way up, so was appropriately proud of his present rank. Like the others, he seemed to view the passengers' hubbub without interest, as though they were just another cargo going to one more port. Handling the excited mob of returnees was our team's problem, not his.

I retired that first evening to a comfortable bunk in my personal cabin on the boat deck, probably the radioman's shack. Its door faced inward toward the big funnel rising through the deck. It was matched on the other side, the starboard side, by the cabin occupied by one of the two Johns. Everyone else was in the main deckhouse. "Good duty," I thought silently, "good food, good quarters, good mattress, and a life of travel to exotic locales."

Next morning we breakfasted as we arose. We spent the day again counting, checking, sorting and moving around passengers and their baggage. I was getting the knack of this. The deck was well filled with more or less comfortable Chinese enjoying the sun and, probably, not working. Quite a few were smoking or playing board games, and even more were cooking food or drying rags on the ship's network of steam pipes along the decks. This steam powered the winches and pumps. Many oriental aromas drifted about, some of them potent. As we got under way that evening, a pervading stink of dried fish blew in through every porthole.

We steamed slowly outward across Manila Bay. I became aware of the slush-his; slush-hiss made by that big triple-expansion steam engine located three decks below my cabin door. The thumping splashes of the bronze propeller blades announced our light loading. Nearly half the prop was above water, so the blades were plunging back into the sea at about one rotation a second. Next I began to sense the assorted rattles, clicks, squeaks and moans from the hull. These were comforting noises to read by as I sailed toward slumber land.

Looking back, it does not seem that I did much real work on this voyage, though my every day was busy. All the rest of the staff knew their jobs and did them methodically. After three years of trying to anticipate problems and solve them quickly, I found this activity pleasant.

Our ship's arrival at Amoy was routine. As we approached, a small Chinese-looking and very smoky tugboat brought out a local pilot to con us in. He was plumply arrayed in a double-breasted blue serge suit, a black wide-brimmed fedora, and scuffed black oxfords. His black framed glasses matched his glistening hair and eyes. Taking over the bridge, he slowly edged us in to an anchoring point in the middle of the wide, shallow harbor. We were not feeling crowded, for the only other motorized ship, nearer the north shore, was a U.S. Navy fleet oiler. The pilot said she had been the first foreign ship since the Japanese took over the area, and that we were the first ship with passengers in nearly ten years. He knew all about our passengers and spoke to some.

A fleet of sampans swept out and surrounded us. Every one, it seemed, had bargains to sell or trade as they milled about and circled our tall-sided ship. Many were family affairs, with several generations helping or shyly peeking from under low shelters. All the people were thin, but then they were poor. I thought of our often-obese underprivileged Americans back home. Different.

The final stamp on our arrival came with a motorized harbor patrol boat cruising in to drive most of the sampans away. That was followed by the slow unfolding of the boarding ladder, or steps, and winching down of a pontoon landing stage alongside it. After several sailors ran up and down making adjustments, the sponsor came on deck with his servants and slowly descended to board the official boat. Many bags and boxes followed, until the whole little troop was ready to leave, opening the way for orderly disembarking of the rest of the passengers as the craft swept away toward the city piers.

Small passenger boats, mostly man-powered, now began to surround us again, ready to take off groups of passengers as they moved down the gangway onto the float. No one was noticeably in charge, but the chaos continually resolved itself as the folks on the outside of the float hopped onto the shore boats and were carried off, all talking. No one checked the manifests. All we did was help as needed and keep some order in the lines of eager passengers. Unloading took far less time, although it seemed to me we disembarked more passengers than we had sent into the holds at Manila. Later I discovered this was quite typical of our ferrying people about.

Later in the afternoon the skipper and our troop commander set off in one of the Snavely's boats to report at the regional admiral's office on the waterfront. The rest of us military and off-duty merchant crew lounged around drinking coffee and observing the harbor activities. A small guard monitored the ship for unauthorized visitors sneaking aboard.

We learned that this admiral was an important public figure in charge of a long strip of coastline, the Fukien Province Amoy naval district. His navy was a fleet of swift armed junks which patrolled constantly against smugglers and pirates. I enjoyed their maneuvering at speed as they sailed in and out, traveling in pairs. True, the hull design was square and boxy. What at a glance had appeared to be square-rigged sails were really more of a lateen rig permitting great maneuverability. Those craft were by no means clumsy. I took several small photos to use in painting views when I got home. And so the day and voyage ended, with little cooking fires aboard river craft winking red after sunset, at Amoy.

Next morning, the Snavely was quiet without its constantly-moving passengers. We hung at anchorage, with only a few salespeople's sampans and several water taxis maintaining position about us, waiting patiently, a state to which they seemed well suited.

After a leisurely breakfast, which was delicious without any aroma of cooking fish, we dressed in khakis in preparation for our required call at the Chinese admiral's waterfront headquarters office. This official reception was a great honor to us. As simple company-grade officers, Americans could expect at most a slight bow and a few ceremonial phrases from some subordinate bureaucrat. This unusual event would give big face to all three parties involved: The U.S.A., the Admiral, and the sponsor of the mass homecoming, so we were all dolled up. The skipper, the mate, and we four soldiers made up the U.S. delegation. Even the coxs'n and crew of our ship's boat looked presentable.

Promptly at eleven we tied up to the admiral's long and wide wharf at riverside. The shore edge was rimmed by a lengthy office building of two stories, with an upper veranda overlooking the harbor traffic. Near the center was the admiral's suite. We were ushered onto the shaded deck and invited to be seated in a row of rocking chairs near the railing. The carefully-aligned chairs made me think of the old ladies' home in Penn Yan, where the elderly residents used to watch me walking past to first grade, constantly rocking in similar chairs on a narrow side porch. We sat.

Rising to greet the admiral when he finally strolled out, we were presented to his Excellency in order of rank. Each American exchanged a series of bows, nodding, smiles, and murmured pleasantries with the local officials. The skipper and transport commander were introduced by name and title, the rest of us simply by rank. Being the final junior, I had ample time to prepare myself for the ceremonious moment.

Next we sat in our assigned chairs and silently rocked for some ten minutes. Stewards appeared with large glasses of hot tea for us to sip as the senior leaders visited politely and honored each other. Their conversation moved erratically, interrupted while interpreters translated the back-and-forth. There was much political laughter. Ceremony in China can take a while.

We onlookers were plied with more tea as quickly as we emptied our glasses. Thus I learned three things: effective ceremony takes a slow pace, consumption of food and drink is ritual, and having been brought up to devour food and drink quickly is painfully wrong in such circumstances. I was the first to request the location of a men's room. Even the answer to this simple request was delayed while a waiter went off to find out what I had asked for.

Finally I was escorted discreetly to the toilet, and there left to my own needs. I was standing alone in the broad entrance to a big room. It was about 25 by 30 feet, and I now wonder if feng shui principles had been observed. It was decoratively tiled on walls and floor, with a colorful wainscoting strip topped by dragons, temple and shipping scenes all round. There were no stalls or stools in the barren space, just marble split trenches neatly aligned near the far wall. Peering down through one of the squat toilets I could see the river sliding smoothly seaward. Each of the side tiles in the floor featured a giant footprint for guidance. It was all fancy; there were no signs telling users to flush after use or to wash hands before returning to duty. I shrugged, did what I had come there for, and returned thoughtfully to rejoin the others in their rocking.

The adjutant told us we were invited to a state dinner as guests of the admiral himself. Only five of us could attend. The first mate had to return to the ship to arrange liberty for crew members. The rest of us waited quietly until about four o'clock, when the admiral's personal car came down to carry us uptown to a fine restaurant. The chief translator explained in detail. I would enjoy a new experience, for the only good Chinese restaurant I'd ever been in was a black lacquer and white tablecloth, red napkin place in Rochester, New York when I was about eight years old. This promised to be even better.

The late afternoon ride up to the restaurant was also memorable. The admiral's touring car was giant, an early 1900's style of the sort the Kaiser rode in. With 36-inch disk wheels, a klaxon horn mounted at the driver's side, a steering wheel fit for an inter-city bus and a canvas touring top and open sides so we could see and be seen, the behemoth was unmarred olive drab and rumbled loudly. As my Grandma Maggie would have said, we were a sight to see.

The wide main business street was filled with pedestrians, cyclists, and rickshaws, plus a few donkeys, ponies and goats. Vendor booths lined the curb areas, but all activity stopped as we approached. The uniformed driver impassively tooted the loud klaxon across the sudden silence.

Every intersection was controlled by a white-gloved, white helmeted police officer. Standing on small platforms centered in the traffic, they waved arms and blew shrill whistles to halt cross traffic, then waved our staff car through without delay. They saluted, and we saluted back. I never saw another motor vehicle in Amoy.

We stopped in the middle of the street, mid-block, and were ushered into the restaurant. The banquet room was on the second floor. Its decor made the Rochester restaurant of my boyhood seem like some remembered roadside diner. At five, we started a many-course meal (some counted forty), a banquet which included a "Gom Bei" toast before, after, and sometimes during each course. Each toast required a standing response and the downing of thimble-size glasses of warm alcohol. The repetitive standing, sitting and swallowing produced a menacing cumulative effect, particularly on innocents like me. Every course was named and explained by a translator for the benefit of us heathens. Thousand-day eggs; bird's nest and snail spit soup; monkey and dog, artfully flavored; fruits and vegetables and seaweed, on and on, thankfully in small quantities but in endless variety, were served by the uniformed waiters. I thought the lights were dimming and flickering.

The solemnity was suddenly inter-rupted. Out of nowhere appeared a tall, thin Chinese in a black robe, his folded arms tucked into deep sleeves. On his head a black felt hat obscured his features as he bowed and bounded about around the skipper's table, stuttering Chinese-sounding syllables. As the skipper and the transport commander struggled up from their chairs, he swept off the hat to reveal himself as our first mate, to the laughter of the entire party. Though swiftly forgiven, he was hustled over to our junior staff table to be silenced.

By midnight the party began to dissolve. The admiral went home in his car, leaving his guests to find their way back to the ship. One of the John lieutenants, the occupant of the other cabin on boat deck, took me in tow as we worked our way through the street level bars to the waterfront. When we reached the wharf it was vacant. The final shore boat was gone, a puzzlement. "Sampan," I think my drinking companion said, as he began hollering and waving his arms at one of the little boats out on the river. The driver held well away from the wharf until he saw a fistful of paper money being waved, then sculled in to let us stumble into the craft. Once seated, we pointed out at the small twinkling lights of our ship way out there in the black water. After more interaction and more money, he began to scull us out toward the Snavely. Accelerating as the outgoing tide took us swiftly past the boarding ladder and on toward Quemoy and Matsu, he fought to control our progress, finally discovering he could not get us back to our ship.

The muscular peasant eventually eased us in toward the north shore where he could paddle slowly against the lessened tidal currents. When we came to the Navy oiler, he swung us alongside and pointed to a ladder hanging over the stern quarter, making signs that this was the end of our ride. As the guard came to peer down at us we tried to explain our plight. Eventually they allowed the two of us to climb aboard, then hustled us into the crew's mess. After restorative cups of black coffee, we were tucked into bunks until dawn. All in all ours had been a great rescue and a friendly recovery.

Our rousting out next morning was pleasant only by comparison with the dressing down we drunken idiots received from the oiler's captain for boarding his ship without first requesting his personal permission. He was not interested in apologies or explanations as he threatened to convict, imprison and try us, in that order. After the initial blast, he went at us again, this time ordering us instead to report to our commanding officer on the Snavely for appropriate action, preferably demotion and possibly cashiering from the service. At last he ran out of steam and dispatched us, without breakfast or coffee, to be repatriated to the Snavely by motor launch.

We were greeted by our troop commander, who found our story even funnier than had been the mate's performance last evening. Off and on during the day, lights came blinking from the oiler toward our bridge, but our signalman was ashore or asleep, so the messages were never acknowledged from our ship.

In the afternoon we started loading passengers for Formosa, or Taiwan as it is now called. By the following day, we had taken aboard more than seven hundred returnees. These were slave laborers who had been lifetime Taiwan residents before being grabbed and shipped to the mainland by the Japanese. This seemed most peculiar to me, for Japan had administered Formosa since 1895, and the residents were, culturally, more like Japanese than Chinese. They had been subjected to a harsh colonial rule, but were better housed, fed, and educated than the mainland residents. Most of the Chinese immigration over the centuries had been individuals and groups fleeing from mainland China. They had intermarried with Malay aborigines, and to some extent with their Japanese conquerors. Now they were going home, and would have a new opportunity to seek solutions there.

The rest of this voyage was routine. We made the hundred-mile crossing through the Straits of Formosa, unloaded our human cargo at the harbor of Taipei, filled up with happy Filipinos, and took them back to Manila regardless where they'd been before abduction. I was beginning to realize how many of these people were not what they'd seemed; they were not laborers and simple peasants. Most were persons who had held leadership roles in their home communities, and were put to common tasks as prisoners, both to break their spirits and to weaken their home communities.

Herman S. Snavely's One-Way Trip

The Herman S. Snavely lay out in the Manila Harbor sun, basking in the airs of a light northerly breeze and cleansed of all signs of the 2,400 steerage passengers. It was good to think of so many uprooted people replanted in their communities, and I wondered what some might be doing. For several days I too basked and loafed as we awaited orders, expecting another full load of returnees to the mainland or someplace new. I was getting a deckhand's tan, but gaining weight.

The skipper's return led to an officers' meeting. The troop commander gravely told us that we were booked to Japan itself. Along the way, we'd drop off a small contingent of American Red Cross workers at Okinawa, which was right on the route, but would carry no other passengers. Just about twenty passengers and a hundred tons of their supplies would be dropped off at Okinawa. Then we would proceed without delay to Tokyo. There we would, surprise!, turn the ship over to the Japs to keep.

"Why? What happens to the ship? What happens to us? What's going on? Why?" We were jolted into asking unmilitary questions.

"We'll be flown back to the Philippines by the Air Force, so don't bring much with you. The Japs need the ship to bring home their armies and civilians from Manchuria, first, but all over East Asia, so things will settle down. In Manchuko alone, that is Manchuria again now, there are several hundred thousand, and some have been there since 1931. Taiwan," (where, I had read, Japanese troops alone totaled 170,000, and civilians as many more) "all these folks are stranded, so a lot of troopers will be needed, and the Japanese fleet of invasion ships is sunk. They'll probably jam a couple thousand on this ship every load."

This would be more than a humanitarian gesture to the defeated enemy, I realized. Such quantities of beaten, bored, and hated troops could be a major danger to the native populations. The logistics of keeping them fed and cooped up would require our troops and all of their backup. And millions of dollars. I could not imagine the scale of this need, compared with little Europe. At least their people could walk home. We should look forward to being out of a job here.

Several landing craft came out. The ship's cranes lifted bulging cargo nets up high, then swung and deposited pallets, supplies and baggage into holds three and four. Some more American food came aboard for this voyage; these passengers would expect at least two hot meals a day. We'd be spared the fishy smell, a good thought. The Navy gun crew quarters on the aft deck were big enough to house the whole group, with the women in the officers section, as I remember.

Like our other trips, we could expect them to be all over the main deck most days. We'd just need to keep them from poking into dangerous places, off the bridge and out of the crew's quarters and engine room. A nice little vacation, oh yes.

Outside, we struck a course northward in the China Sea, and word got around that we would be edging into a typhoon before we came to Okinawa. One of these I had not seen before, but I'd heard about them: tracking north-westerly out of the Pacific, winds up to 100 knots or more, seas of thirty to forty feet, horizontal salt rain, and ships driven ashore, or broken or turned over, all common enough. Why worry?

Here the tropical breeze was balmy, and we created our own airflow at a steady nine knots, some 250 miles a day. Just a slight rising motion across the gentle diagonal swells which signify a calm Pacific Ocean. Who would not enjoy such leisure?

When we plowed out of the protection of Taiwan's bulk, the interlude was over. Even at reduced speed, we were not going to avoid some part of this storm, though it was nowhere nearly as terrifying as the one which had swung disaster into Okinawa and the Ryukyu island chain about a year before. We encountered rough wave action and ever-stronger gusts. The Liberty Ship rode high in ballast, subject to every change in wind pressure as she rolled and wallowed. By dark, the high-riding propeller and rudder were popping out of the sea as the bow plunged down and the stern bounced up. This added surges and vibration to the yawing and diving which soon sent our bellies into convolutions. We were not very deep into the storm, but it was roaring across our plotted course. Our passengers were already uniting in seasickness and many sought refuge on the boat deck after the bridge.

At dinner, the plate rails were on our table in the officers' mess. Soup and beverages were half-filled as the steward served them very carefully. The menu was simple and rather bland, as I remember. Shortly, I sought my little cabin on the boat deck to brace myself and read. The built-in bunk's high wooden sides, almost crib-like, let me brace myself diagonally as I slept rather fitfully. I did not worry about the passengers. They were all trained by the Red Cross.

The weather did not get worse as we trailed the massive storm northward, though the wave structure increased our rolling to about forty degrees each side. It is strange to look straight out past the rail at angry green sea water being lashed into froth and sprayed into your unprotected eyes. Our speed was down to five knots, and the wheelsman up front was spinning spokes constantly trying to maintain course. I was glad I was not too worried. We were in the hands of seamen who had been out here before.

Over a day or so the storm passed off toward Korea, the seas subsided, and the rolling became almost comfortable. We chugged on at ten knots, making up time, seeing no one, until at last we came up on the West beaches of Okinawa. We had made our designated port. This was the same place the errant typhoon had come through to wreck so many ships. The beach remained littered with the debris of that greater storm. There was no pier awaiting us, so we anchored out a ways and awaited orders.

In due time a small fleet of landing craft, LCVPs and LCTs came out. These were boxy, flat-bottomed vessels, all open deck for equipment and supplies. Imagine a sea-going wheelbarrow. The Snavely's cranes were unlimbered to swing the tonnage over the side in short order. The Red Cross people lined the rail, watching and bitching about the bumpy seas and having to get to shore. They envisioned having to climb down swaying ladders, or worse. But it was so much easier. The crew gently dropped some of the last filled cargo nets to the deck, helped the passengers climb on the net, and then simply dropped them into the waiting boats before they had time to complain. No one fell off or screamed loudly. We did not wait to see them land on the beach.

Quickly getting back to sea, our ship soon turned northward again, and this time keeping off east of the Ryukyus, up Honshu to Tokyo Bay. Here a pilot boarded and took us serenely into the great Yokosuka Naval Base, where two oriental-looking, very tiny black tugboats with tall slender funnels nudged the Snavely smoothly in to a wharf beneath a tall rock cliff. The narrow dockage was bordered by railroad tracks running deep into the caves the Japs had created as bomb shelters, to provide safe harbor for the Home Fleet which no longer existed. I again was happy that this war was over.

Off us military types went, with goodbyes all around, for we were ordered to a replacement camp outside Yokohama. We left the merchant crew aboard to keep house until they were sent elsewhere. Probably they would spend a few days breaking a Japanese crew into the ship's systems.

Soon we were boarding an express train at a battered Tokyo railroad station. This sleek silver snake seemed completely untouched, like a Buck Rogers machine on some wrecked planet. We sat in comfort, looking out large sealed windows as the quiet train accelerated smoothly to its inter-city speed of a hundred kilometers an hour. The shining rails were smooth and noiseless as we whistled through what had recently been Japan's industrial and commercial heartland.

I might have been looking at Hiroshima. The tattered, shattered landscape stretched far out of sight. Only an occasional broken factory chimney or a cluster of broken-off and bent steel girders protruded above the flattened, fire-eaten ruins. As we rushed on toward Yokahama, we saw only a slow cyclist, a few standing pedestrians, along the road beside us. Dante would have found the scene real.

This was Desolation. Worse, it had not been the single blast of a super-bomb which had killed this city-after-city. Fire had done it. We had sent flight upon flight of long-range super bombers to drop fire bombs and explosives, creating conflagrations which fed upon themselves. Unstoppable fire-storms flared on until there was no more to burn. Those who had died under the big new bombs had found a better death.

We were serious and polite as we detrained, an hour later, in the Yokohama terminal. I wondered if the survivors of all this knew how fortunate they had been when their empire's leaders at last surrendered.

We didn't get around much in the three days until we were booked on a flight back to the Philippines for reassignment. The four-motored cargo plane was huge compared with any aircraft I had previously flown in. Although the seats were metal and the surroundings spartan, I felt fairly at ease as we rumbled down the long bomber runway. All engines were at full power. This was our air force plane and crew. I settled down for the long flight over gently rolling silver and blue seas, napping and awakening fully as the pilots lowered the wheels and flaps to land back home. Ha! I was thinking of this as home!

Into the Boondocks in an LCI

My every return to AFWESPAC headquarters in Manila brought me a new job. This next one emerged quickly and soon proved "a wild and crazy thing." I left the personnel office with the Military Specialty Number of Troop Transport Commander, my designation now long lost by my memory as well as the official army file system. (You may recall that the War Department's depository in St. Louis burned shortly after WWII, destroying all duty and promotion records of most veterans.)

In my new authority, as in most army jobs, there was a catch. No, there were two. I became Troop Transport Commander on a Landing Craft, Infantry — an LCI with a merchant marine crew. This was a ship with no name, just a number. The LCI's were numerous, small and too expendable to rate names, I guess. Secondly, I was in command of what the new army recruiting slogan calls "a team of one." I was alone. The merchant crew was civilians running the boat. I was The Army, the passenger agent, cruise director, and official if sometimes uncertain voice of General MacArthur when making things happen or stopping things which were not to happen. I remembered that I was also still a first lieutenant with a single silver bar and neither experience nor precedent to guide me.

We'd be operating the seagoing equivalent of a Manila jitney service in this new scheme. Someone upstairs, and probably some committee, had noticed how effective the jitney buses were, and determined that a small, fairly fast, shallow draft boat could slip into landings not reachable easily from the Liberty Ships. The LCI-type could easily shift small bunches of indigenous personnel in and out of the same coastal landing beaches used by native outrigger canoes. Our clientele would number 200 or less, and usually far less. Our trips would be only a day or two's duration. It would all be inter-island, of course. The Philippines is a sea full of 7,100 volcanic islands and islets, with waterways the national highways. I have long suspected that I was the only officer doing this experiment, though of course no one told me. My orders were unspecific, as usual. Just make this work.

My driver and I eventually located LCI 316 (or some such number, I forget) among a long row of such cloned invasion craft. They were tethered together, beached, in a remote part of the back lot. Only the numbers distinguished individual LCI's, as far as I could tell. Only later did I learn that not all were infantry landing craft as originally designed. Some were mine-sweepers, others gunboats, some flak boats, some ammo carriers. But mine was the original troop carrier, and up close it did look bigger than those I'd seen at a distance.

LCI 316 was only 160 feet in length — about one-third the length of the Snavely, and it was narrow, just a bit more than 20 feet in beam. With a draft of only five feet, four inches at the bow, and five feet, eleven inches at the stern (please remember this figure), getting into primitive ports and over shallow bottoms would be simple. Or not difficult. Powerful General Motors diesels, two pair, totaling 1,600 horsepower, turned twin shafts with variable pitch propellers. Its assets were a top speed of 16 knots — some 20 miles per hour — and the maneuverability possible only with two props. We could water ski, basically. Her four 20mm guns had been removed, I could see, but the big emergency life rafts still hung in their racks, and the long infantry landing ramps were housed next to the gunnels. With its low profile, the main deck for troops was only about six feet above the waterline. The one tall projection was the armored con tower which served as the bridge. An LCI looked much like a surfaced submarine from a distance.

No gangplank watch showed up as I walked up the extended landing ramp and looked toward the deckhouse. I could hear the loud accented voice of one man, but saw no one until I came upon the captain just inside the con tower. He was very angry and I hoped not his usual self. He was cursing

Finns and all Finnish sailors, if I understood this. Another one of them had pulled a knife "from behind head like dom' coward," he gestured, simply because the sailor had come aboard drunk again, and the captain had summarily discharged him. He'd thrown him overboard into the shallow water and wished he had killed the guy.

The skipper's tirade next turned to 'Trumpeeters' and his concern that I might be one of those. A brass horn-playing Trumpeeter had stolen his wife, his daughter, or his girlfriend. The captain did not seem too sure, but I understood he "wos dom' mod." He remained upset as he turned and disappeared into his cabin, slamming the door. Well!

I found the mate, a good-looking American about 25 years old, and heard that the skipper was a peace-time bosun of Norwegian ancestry, a good seaman if sober and calm, and his own biggest problem in this, his first command. I felt my situation might be just bearable.

"The captain thinks the mate and I are trying to steal all the charts and navigation instruments," volunteered a husky guy who turned out to be the engineer, the only other officer aboard. "Skipper keeps the charts on navigation locked up in his cabin, and he just put the fire axes in there too. He sure doesn't trust anybody." (Only the captain's cabin had a door; the other officers had hall doorways with sliding curtains.)

At least they both knew our orders. As soon as the troop commander arrived, LCI 316 was to proceed to Legaspi to pick up a Filipino Army platoon, and deliver it back to Manila. North of Legaspi, nearer the base of Mount Mayon, and not a port, just a landing place at a cove at the end of dirt road. More of a track than a road. Out in the boondocks.

An explanation and translation: Boondocks is an Americanization of the Filipino words "bun dok" which means "wilderness" or more specifically "mountains" originally. Mount Mayon is the islands' tallest active volcano, a perfect cone with the fumes drifting out of the top dropping a bit of ash and a sniff of sulfur fumes downwind. Mayon has erupted every few years as long as men have watched it, about 45 major eruptions since 1616. It is the top of the Sierra Madre, Eastern Luzon's coastal range where primitive tribesmen still live. Easy to spot. Just ask anybody. So we'd better shove off.

So we did, after the mate got the captain's drowsy approval. We left after I shooed off a few transients, friends, and relatives who wished to go along for the ride. The deck crew pulled in both ramps and secured them while the engine crew started the main engines. Stirring up clouds of mud as the propellers churned, we backed out with a giant sucking sound from the mudflat, rotated on our axis, and proceeded out through the familiar harbor route to the sea. We then turned generally south before sunset, about a mile off from the shore. As it got dark abruptly, tropic-style, I could see that tree line fading into blackness to our left. Our running lights were the only lights I could make out, until the stars began to wink on.

I joined the mate and the engineer, who were talking quietly on the con bridge. It was true, not a chart or reference table in sight, only the ship's compass, which was not transportable. No dividers, no ruler, no chronometer. Everything else was directly below us, locked in the captain's cabin along with the skipper. Available only by mutiny, which would be a dumb idea. Again, I was thankful for the LCI's shallow draft, its maneuverability, and the keen eyes of our bow lookout, the steersman, and the two officers.

We navigated visually, from point to point in the starlight. They spoke of the necessary clearance and the remembered names for various points. There were no navigational aids, no buoys or lighthouses. The only shoreline lights were occasional beach fires, for these were country areas, jungles and forests without roads to require headlights. What might have been available had been stripped away by the Japanese in anticipation of MacArthur's return. I hoped dawn would break before we made our turn eastward around the southern tip of Luzon. I decided to turn in.

As I remember events, it was two or three quiet and uneventful days later before the captain appeared, ready to take us in for landing. We were past Legaspi, abeam the giant lava cone with its long plume drifting off to invisibility westward. We edged slowly inward diagonally to the shore, seeking the entrance to a small cove, the mouth of one of the little rivers descending from the interior. Alongside the northern bank appeared a narrow wharf adjoining a dirt one-track road. About a mile of jungle separated us from the bottom of Mount Mayon. There must be a village in there; this area was reportedly well populated.

Docking should be easy. We could simply idle in, reverse engines with port rudder to swing in the stern, and tie up alongside. Even I knew that from my Keuka Lake boating days.

Apparently the captain didn't. From the deck, I marveled as we started, stopped, maneuvered, backed down, and went forward again trying to come alongside the wharf. Finally, the deckhands jumped onto the dock and snubbed our heavy manila hawsers around posts. After bow, stern and spring lines were in place, and engines were stopped, the mate told me we had both propeller shafts, six feet under water, wrapped tightly with the trailing ends of those two-inch hempen hawsers. The sodden lines would have to be cut away, piece by piece, before the ship could move again.

The captain ordered the engineer and the mate to fix the problem, and strongly recommended that I join them, as only officers could be trusted with the knives. I was glad for my summers of swimming as I got ready to take a look.

There wasn't any diving equipment available. We would have to free-dive six feet down, another eight under the stern, and cut away the lines with the cook's largest kitchen knives. The tangle could not be undone by hand. It had to be cut from both shafts — a real mess.

It was fortunate that we were all decent swimmers, young and in good shape. Only one person at a time dared work on each shaft in the murky river water. We could not stay down long enough to chop away very much at a dive. Rigging lines did help, but we tired of holding on with one hand, fighting our own buoyancy while wielding a knife in the other for as long as we could hold our breath. The hemp was wet and tough, and we had to work slowly to sever a few strands at a time. It took us three wearisome days to hack free the lines so they could be pulled out. Then we were free to go back to our day jobs, without thanks and with enough of underwater exploration to know we were glad to be in the Army.

We waited there several more days without complaint, at least three of us enjoying the change. Before we left, the peace was interrupted when the cook asked the captain's permission to trade some food stores. One of the ships in Legaspi had a lot of Indonesians in their crew who were grousing because the ship had no rice left. Their cook was radioing around looking to trade potatoes for rice, because they would not eat the potatoes. We had no potatoes left, but surplus bags of rice. This would make us a good deal, he said expectantly. We'd have potatoes to serve instead of eternal infernal rice.

"Let them eat their own Goddam' potatoes!" shouted the captain. "They don't get my rice!" and he stomped off into his cabin. His fuse was getting shorter.

Four rattling surplus army trucks came down the narrow track full of Philippine Army troops and gear. A captain and two lieutenants ordered them around and eventually aboard. For some reason the scene made me think of George Washington dealing with colonial militia soldiers. I got them settled down, told them it would be about three days to get in to Manila, and set up details with their commander. Their only shelter was a canvas awning stretched over the deck; food would be U.S. rations, and lots of that rice. All their ammo was turned in and guarded. Just routine stuff.

We fumbled our way back to Manila, rocking and pitching along the edge of a tropical storm for two days as we followed it up the west coast of Luzon past those same points and bays we'd passed before. The troops did not seem to notice the way we were navigating. Perhaps it was what they expected. I was beginning to think such predicaments were normal. So we landed with no problems, ramping the soldiers down to the beach where they collected their gear and were marched off at route step, not singing.

Where Are You, John Masefield?

When I reported in at Manila headquarters I hoped I'd be assigned to some other transportation duty; perhaps a safari someplace.

Reality prevailed. In a weird way. I was "promoted" again. I'd been assigned as troop commander on a Liberty Ship. It would shuttle around the Philippines carrying people. On these short inter-island runs, all passengers would essentially be deck cargo; families, smaller units of the Filipino armed forces, regulars and militia traveling the sea road to new assignments.

If the LCI had been a jitney, the Cyrus J. Polansky would be more like a commuter bus on a country line. I visualized the once-a-day-each-way local which traveled from Geneva, New York southward to Penn Yan, Branchport, Hammondsport, and Bath with passengers and packages, a slow but respectable way to serve the rural areas. I would be the conductor, not the driver. I would also be alone again, the sole U.S. Army official representative with a Merchant Marine crew operating the ship. I was sure the food and quarters would be good.

No mention was made of the LCI-316 boondocker. I was not de-briefed. I do not remember receiving official paperwork, transfer orders or written directions. Not a word passed between me and any AFWESPAC brass. The concept had proved unworkable. Control and organization systems would be necessary beyond any practicality, I believe. I did not offer to factor in the craziness buried in the sample.

By now I had developed a real liking for these different voyages, for being at sea and for being a lone operator. I decided to put in a formal request for my upcoming trip back to the States, assignment as a security officer aboard some cargo ship taking the southern route through the Panama Canal, to New York. Some army officers were being sent as supercargoes on vessels leaving Manila for East Coast U.S. ports.

Knowing my return to the States would be only a month or two away, I contacted the personnel section which incidentally handled such orders, and put in my request. I looked forward to lazing through several weeks in the Southern Seas, the Canal, the Caribbean Sea, and arriving both rested and well fed at, say, a Jersey City pier.

My hopes actually brightened when I saw the nameplate of the officer's desk. A captain, and a Jensen. He may have been Henry or Hiram, some "H" name. "Just a little something extra in the bank," I muttered as I strode out. (This comforting glow persisted until I at last came to claim the prize: I found out the captain had booked himself home and departed on my vacation trip, leaving no instructions behind.)

For now, I happily switched to the Cyrus J. Polansky. This Liberty Ship was an even simpler conversion of the cargo vessel. Perhaps the "accommodations" had been done here, in preparation for the short run to Honshu. The Merchant Marine crew members evidenced attitudes that they'd been out here a while. A little too long, I guessed. I met the two mates and a pair of engineering officers who did seem steady and even glad to see me in place for this new shuttle service. The ship's captain was ashore, according to the first mate.

At mess, my new companions explained that the Polansky's captain enjoyed his position and status, but did have a few eccentricities. I needed to know about such factors in order to function, of course. Their reluctance to expand on these peculiarities worried me, but I would have to discover them for myself. The food was good, my little cabin was fine, and all ship shape and Bristol fashion, as the old saying goes. We had radio contact with Manila Dispatch from the Polansky and would be routed from port to port. This was a big improvement.

Another asset was the LCVP cradled atop hatch number four. The adaptable Landing Craft Vehicle and Personnel could be swung over side to provide pickup and delivery service where the Liberty had to anchor out for lack of depth or dockage. The clumsy-looking LCVP could push its nose into a beach, drop a ramp, and back off with a deck-full of passengers and baggage. That would be far better than using local canoes and fishing craft at island villages.

Obviously the system was maturing. As we moved slowly among the maze of mountainous islands making up the Commonwealth, we gradually relocated families and private citizens as well as troop units and numerous officials. We touched here and there where there were no roads to anywhere. The Philippines were moving toward recovery; such ships as ours provided free transportation.

The wandering of the Cyrus J. appeared aimless at times as we idled along like a bus at the end of its route. We puttered everywhere, it seemed, except to the long-fingered island of Palawan off at the southwest perimeter of the group. Days flowed uncounted, though no two were alike. Some few deserve re-telling.

As the troop commander I officially decided who could board the Polansky for free travel. This was a valued privilege that often required on-the-spot negotiation. The radio order simply authorized us to transport Major So-and-so or Colonel Surname "and family," without names listed, or numbers either. I had quickly learned "and family" was a portmanteau term in this society. Family meant sisters and brothers, uncles and aunts, cousins by the dozens. Each sub-family brought its own retainers. The retainers brought their families. All brought their pets and household animals. Chickens and ducks could not be abandoned. They came aboard, as did more limited numbers of goats, sheep and porkers. By using the LCVP, we could carry a reasonable amount of animals and their feed for short voyages. Crew would daily sluice off the droppings with seawater.

The passengers could care for their menagerie. Fair enough, most times.

The army officers proudly wore their American dress uniforms with insignia of rank and service bars. Some expected VIP treatment I could not make available. Most were field grade or generals, as I remember. I had seen few lieutenants traveling.

One lieutenant colonel created a substantial problem. He presented himself ready to board with two water buffalo in his train. The big, black, scimitar-horned carabao have to be cooled at least several times a day, and we had no pools or showers for them. They also must eat heartily and they produce a commensurate amount of juicy fertilizer. They may be good-natured but are not, to my mind, loveable. The deck-hands would rebel and might be injured. I was unreasonable. We went round and round before his adjutant agreed to leave the two beasts with more of the colonel's local relatives. The colonel offered to report me through official channels. He had calmed down before he went down the gangway two days later.

As we steamed about, the Cyrus J. Polansky took on a persistent aroma of fish being cooked on steam pipes, excrement, and smoked everything. A barn-like stink pervaded my ark.

I enjoyed the friendly weather we moved through those days. Blue skies were studded with small puffball clouds over the islands. The notoriously temperamental China Sea waved gently day and night, and all our passengers stayed on deck. As I moved among them, they shared smiles and grins. Crewmembers off watch sunned themselves in restricted areas.

I raised my eyes from this peace to notice the captain on the bridge. He was accompanied by a brace of longhaired young Filipinas. Their brief, tight, bright dresses blazed against the gray paint all around them. I thought them too young to be traveling alone.

"Old Skipper always has a couple of them gals aboard with him," commented the second mate. "Keeps him from getting nervous and lonesome." He grinned. This was one of the captain's unmentioned eccentricities. The girls stayed up there in officer country. When the skipper sought pleasures ashore, they waited patiently in his quarters. He left and returned alone, often at late hours.

This captain didn't look like a ladies' man. He was stubby, rotund, with short legs, unhandsome but not ugly. His ruddy cheeks and nose, like his eye-whites, seemed not the products of mere years at sea. His casual, laid-back ways of management I now attributed to a personally planned early retirement program. On the other hand he was clean shaven and neatly barbered. Properly uniformed, showing manicured nails on his small pudgy fingers, he was innocuous.

"Wait until the full of the moon," commented my informant. "He stands out on the end of the bridge and bays at the moon.

Real loud, too." I knew the sailor was pulling my leg, but I didn't let on.

A few nights later the hair rose on the back of my neck as I tensed to a long, mournful howl drifting through my open porthole. Except for usual ship noises the bright midnight had been quiet. I looked out. The gray ship was now silver, the shadows intensely black and knife-sharp. I stood barefoot in my skivvies and stared up at the bridge, watching a stubby, stark-white figure tip back its head to salute the mysterious queen of the heavens with another wordless ululation. My leg had not been pulled. I had a third type of Pacific skipper for my collection.

One of the dramatic photos of the Pacific War symbolizes General MacArthur returning to the Philippines as he had promised. He wades ashore at Leyte. A Landing Ship Tank is behind him, its huge ramp lowered into the surf where his entourage strides raggedly behind him. All are wet to the knees. He is accompanied by President Sergio Osmena of the Philippines and four high-ranking U.S. officers in khakis. On the right, a helmeted staff sergeant carries two slung carbines, one over each shoulder as he plows through the water.

There's a story behind this stirring scene. The great black and white action photo is said to be the second take. The original version was re-enacted, it is said, because the water was too deep. Fresh dry and pressed uniforms were donned while the landing ship pushed into shallower water. The second photo captured the glory for the record, back in January 1945.

I repeated this landing sixteen months later when the Polansky called at Leyte's south shore to pick up refugees. There I heard the MacArthur story, and I believed. The landing spot was next to a pier created by an abandoned assault ship to which our vessel was securely tied. The captain had, however, spun the 441-foot steamer around twice, end for end in the narrow channel, before stopping stern-to-shore against the pier. Amused deckhands had tossed hawsers across the gap to laughing locals as our ship completed its elephantine maneuver.

After that, it seemed completely logical for several of us to mosey out to knee depth and have our pictures taken. Verified by my descendants but no longer extant, the photos captured us wading ashore, MacArthur-style; thanks to the general, however, we only needed one take.

This was a modest high spot in the several weeks we spent in routine service, doing our humble part in put-and-take at many of the named islands. We picked up, and we delivered.

Eventually a message came to steam down to Jolo, the capital of Sulu Province. This port is located near the southwest end of a chain of little islands at the southern limit of the Philippines. A relatively big and undamaged port, Jolo had a wharf at which the Polansky could tie up. We arrived sharply without maneuvers, and the skipper ordered the chief engineer to pull both boilers. This would shut down the Polansky's power completely. We were scheduled to remain in port for several days, pending arrival of a large list of passengers. The engine-room crew would clean the boilers. The captain rode off alone in an open carriage to visit downtown Jolo, a mile or so away on a dusty road.

I'd read articles about the Moros who inhabit the Sulu Islands, tribes of sea-going pirates, expert sailors of lateen-rigged catamarans and reluctant citizens of the Philippines. Mohammedans who had colonized these islands late in Asiatic history, they were Malay in origin and fiercely independent. I had heard how they carried the Kris, a wavy-bladed close-combat fighting knife. Passengers told how all Moros could swim like fish, and had gills like fish as well (I had not seen anyone with gills, but then...). Their name, Moro, is a version of "Moor," from the time of early Spanish rule. To this day, this whole area is life-endangering for Christians and other non-believers.

With its fires out, the big Polansky hung securely hawsered to the wharf, where dozens of ferocious local merchants had materialized to barter with us. Later that afternoon I was engaged in trading two unopened cartons of American cigarettes, probably Camels, for a large stamped brass plate offered by a turbaned red-toothed thief, when the captain arrived in a cloud of dust behind a panting, sweating little horse. I must say the Old Man appeared to be both disheveled and distraught.

"Tell the chief not to pull the damn' boilers!" he hollered up at the third mate, who was on gangplank duty. "We gotta get outta here! Fast! The goddam' Moros are coming!" The mate understood this unusual order, and called down the communication tube to the chief engineer. The chief apparently did not ask any questions either.

As we prepared for hasty departure, some facts became known. The Moros were not chasing the skipper personally nor endangering the Cyrus J. Polansky except incidentally. He had been upstairs downtown when rumor spread that one or more of the Moro chieftains were about to attack, or sack, the city or part of it. Something like that. The city was in a state of alarm, and it was about to be no place for a holiday weekend.

We got up steam in a hurry, headed out to sea and then radioed Manila that no passengers had been made available for pickup.

While I remained aboard the Polansky, neither of her two boilers was drawn down for thorough maintenance, though it may have been done while I was ashore for one week in Manila. This time included the July 1946 Independence Day, a celebration earlier noted in this memoir.

My time for home-going was drawing close, so I again inquired about the possibility of a southern trip assignment as supercargo on a freighter bound for the East Coast. Instead I was sent off to bring back the Cyrus J. Polansky's biggest load yet, from the major island of Panay.

The ship was ordered to dock at the island's principal port of Iloilo pending the arrival of a battalion of PI infantry which had been getting field training in the boonie hills behind that city. The 1,300 soldiers could not be brought down to the riverside port until our vessel's arrival was confirmed to their colonel commanding. Our captain had specific orders to go there and not to leave until the troops were safely aboard. Some informers must have ratted about our abandoning those people down at Jolo, we figured.

The Port of Iloilo was not at the sea, but a mile or more up a river estuary, nicely sheltered from storms on a narrow but deep channel. A big pier ran along the shore, with plenty of depth for the Polansky to pull alongside. The first mate took the big ship slowly upriver, there being no local pilot service. He swung the vessel about so we were docked with the bow pointing out to sea, which seemed a reasonable enough precaution to me.

(A note here: a vessel having two engines and two propellers can maneuver quite easily by using power and reversing one engine. The Liberty Ship, like other single-screw steamers, was more difficult to handle; a combination of tide, river currents, wind, and restricted turning room could make professional handling essential.)

At that time Iloilo did not see many large passenger vessels at its docks, so our arrival was treated as a special occasion. We were honored at an evening reception. Our group included our reluctant captain, all of the ship's officers, plus me as troop commander. The formal affair was held at a large home of a city official, elevated a full story above the ground, with a veranda on all sides of the living rooms. We went up a long, broad wooden staircase to the entrance.

The ladies, old and young, wore dress gowns with puffed sleeves which are a national costume. The local men wore casual cotton shirts with slacks, or business suits. The local officials were in appropriate uniform for the formal event. The battalion itself was not represented. It passed through my mind that this celebration might also be occasioned by the pending departure of those infantrymen up in the hills.

We all stood around having punch and cookies, making conversation with the local men. The ladies gathered on the opposite side of the wide room, a pretty but separated group. The party was brief, at least for us. We returned to the quiet of the Cyrus J. Polansky before dark, there to wait and wonder what would happen next.

Several quiet, peaceful days passed with no communication from the battalion commander up in the boondocks. Our increasingly irritable skipper announced that the ship would depart on the evening tide two days hence, with or without the troops. I began to sweat. He was the autocrat, the captain. No arguing, no explaining, no matter. This was his ship. I was the supreme troop commander, with no power but full responsibility. Who would catch the blame? I knew.

About 1300 hours, one o'clock in the afternoon of our departure day, I spotted a growing slash of dust rising along the hilltops.

Steadily growing larger, it revealed at its base a long column of GI trucks and semis rolling about 40 miles an hour down toward the dock area. Every truck was full of small and dusty green-clad soldiers complete with arms, knapsacks, and steel helmets.

Silence came as the column pulled up, still in line, and the infantrymen boiled out of the trucks like ants from a stomped ant-hill. Abandoning the rolling stock, they formed up in columns ready to board, and then surged forward. All I could do was stand at the top of the gangplank with two of their officers, directing units forward or aft to make room for the steady rush.

Anything to get them all aboard before the skipper orders us to cast off, I figured. I saw no roll call and received no written manifest, but I was going home from Manila. I reasoned that it was about like the Safe Hand Air Courier Service: I was responsible for the package but not the contents.

Oops!

Suddenly I realized that some of the uniformed soldiers did not walk like men. In the stream, an occasional woman passed, also fully uniformed and armed. Working the rush, females were being smuggled aboard and right down into the holds. I stopped two of them, and bargained with a major: this was not allowed.

"They're nurses, lieutenant," he said, smiling. Okay, I responded, all women would be housed in the nurses' quarters, formerly the Navy guard unit's deckhouse on the stern — under officer supervision. We agreed I would forget any ladies already smuggled. We satisfied the rule if not the principle with about thirty damsels in that deckhouse for the trip. Order prevailed.

In a day or so we cruised quietly into an anchorage far out in Manila Bay and I began my countdown of hours remaining. This trip was safely completed. I'd surely be going home in a week or two.

The quarantine inspector's boat with its yellow "plague" ensign came along side. Public health must be preserved. Inspectors must approve passengers for debarkation. This was some new formality, I assumed.

I was wrong. The senior inspectors met with the captain privately, and then with me present, as they asserted that the Cyrus J. Polansky had yellow fever among the passengers. Up with the yellow "Quarantined" flag and down with any plan for anyone, passenger or crew, to disembark. Quarantine would continue until at least two weeks after the last case of yellow fever had recovered — or died, I supposed. We all were here to stay, including my most important concern, the troop commander. I'd be here for at least sixty to ninety days, watching our troopships pull out for the States. This situation upset me more than it did the captain and his social life.

Again I was inspired to negotiate. I demanded a second, confirming inspection by military doctors, citing the large number of troops. This ship deserved re-inspection. I deserved to go home, too, but I didn't tell them that.

My luck changed once more. These were scattered cases of chickenpox, not the dreaded yellow fever. The yellow flag came down. I was free to go ashore as previously ordered. Taking no further chances, I hitched a ride in with the military inspectors. My orders had specified "immediately upon arrival." I was immediate in carrying them out.

Next day I had orders to go home, and adjourned to the nearby replacement depot with my gear. Life promised to get rational, with no more snafus. Home Again, Home Again!

Having polished off forgettable details in Manila, I shortly received my homeward marching order — sailing orders, really. I'd be just a name on a passenger manifest again, but for a first class cruise through the Southern Seas, I thought to myself. The ship's name was the Marine Dragon.

The Marine Dragon was a C-4B military hospital/troop transport, the longest class of cargo vessel built during World War II by the U.S. Maritime Commission. Five hundred twenty feet at the waterline, she was one of fourteen similar "Marine"-named ships. Her single screw would drive her at seventeen knots – more than 400 miles a day for 12,000 miles. I looked forward to a comfortable trip homeward on the "Dragon Wagon" under sunny skies.

My rosy expectations increased when we were ordered to stow all heavy winter clothing in our hold baggage, retaining only tropical uniforms. Once aboard, my realistic appraisal of military operations was confirmed.

The Marine Dragon pulled out of Manila, but did not turn south. Instead, our bow swung northward as our speed increased. The word soon spread that we were on a great circle route to the north. This would take the ship arctic-ward past Japan and the Kamchatka Peninsula, close to the tip of the Aleutian Islands, then swing southeast toward San Francisco Bay and Oakland.

Brrr!

A number of the guys I'd known were also on the big ship, men from our Infantry School class, from duty stations, and even from ROTC at Syracuse University. On this voyage we did not sit on the deck plates to play cards, for that deck was far too cold, and usually wet. Nor did we speak much of where we'd been or what had happened to us. We talked about our plans for home, our anticipation of civilian life renewed after three or more years' absence in uniform.

We also groused about the final AFWESPAC snafu as we milled about on deck, draped in soggy army blankets trying to keep warm. The overall scene made me think how many of our grandparents had come to the Promised Land in steerage. I was glad for the wool blanket.

Through the extra-long summer days, we stared at the northern ocean. As we passed into American waters, we claimed to have seen one of the Aleutian Islands through the gray mists. We discussed: Was it Attu? Or was it perhaps tiny Agattu, out there at the end of the world? No matter, it was ours.

Our other big event lasted only a few minutes. As we sped along, a large pod of whales appeared on the port side, diving and surfacing with gigantic ease, proving hard to count as they effortlessly paralleled our course, probably watching the ship and feeling its vibrations. Then they swung closer, only to dive beneath the Marine Dragon and be gone.

Fortunately we passed through the Golden Gate in less than half the sea-time consumed by the outward war-time voyage of the Cape Mendocino.

After a year more or less at sea, at 24 years of age I was soon back on dry land for good, and only about three thousand miles from home.

After Words

As I wrote segments of this memoir and shared them with my men's writing group, I was surprised to find how few of these writers, many of them in their sixties, knew about the places, things and events which are so rich in my own only slightly longer memories. Victory versus Liberty Ships, types and identification of landing craft, names and locations of places in the western Pacific were as much in the news as our current coverage of Iraq, Afghanistan, Palestine and Israel. Everyone knew the implements and geography of war with the same familiarity we have today with Baghdad and Blackhawks. Maybe, I began to think, this piece has a purpose other than to give me exercise.

Thanks to the internet, strange things, places and events can be perused in substantial detail. The term "boondocks" for instance, which means "mountains" in Tagalog, is an Americanized term which came out of the Luzon Mountains near

Mayon volcano a century ago when our soldiers were fighting the Philippine insurrectionists. Dutch New Guinea and Hollandia in my story are now Irian Jaya and Jayapura. Amoy and Fukien Province also have new names. The last Liberty Ships are in United States maritime museums. The ancient veterans are disappearing, leaving only their recorded voices, words and some pictures behind.

"More or Less at Sea" is more than a title. It describes where I lived for a long-ago year on the edges of the Far East.

-Al Jensen

July, 2003

Tucson, Tulsa and Santa Barbara

About the Author

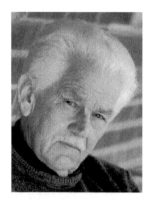 Al Jensen was born Alfred B. Jensen, Jr. in Penn Yan, Yates County, New York. He is a graduate of Penn Yan Academy and was a Denison Scholar at Syracuse University, where he earned both baccalaureate and master's degrees with honors. He enlisted in the U.S. Army in 1942 and was commissioned in 1944. He returned to inactive reserve status as a captain. He worked in local government and with a national volunteer agency before entering private business. His poetry and essays have appeared in anthologies, newspapers and magazines. He writes primarily about the Finger Lakes District of the Empire State, and about the Southwest.

Made in the USA
Charleston, SC
14 February 2011